"Heidi has given to us – and to our daughters – a crucial gift: the shining picture of godly womanhood written for a generation that has been told more lies than we can even imagine. This loving book, clearly and accessibly written, cuts through the d [illegible] nfused world without bel [illegible] ptives. Heidi talks directl [illegible] ct and care. The writing i [illegible] atter is vital. Parents, give [illegible] read it and discuss it with them.

Rosaria Champagne Butterfield, Speaker, Homemaker and Author of *The Secret Thoughts of an Unlikely Convert*

"If I could give any book to myself when I was a younger woman with dreams about love and marriage, it would be this book. Choosing Love casts a deep, wide, and stalwart vision for the purpose of marriage and beautifully invites readers to be a part of a story that is so much bigger than their own. Choosing Love will make your heart beat fast for the beauty God intended to flourish within the context of marriage."

Ellie Holcomb, Dove Award Winning Singer/Songwriter

"I've known Heidi for years, and have seen her love for her family, her church, and her Savior up close. She's the real deal. Amidst all the clamor of the untrue story the world tells us about who we are and who God is, Heidi's voice is a calm, clear, and wise reminder that there's a better, truer story to be told. I can't wait for my daughter to read this book."

Andrew Peterson, Singer/Songwriter and Author of *Adorning the Dark* and *The Wingfeather Saga*

CHOOSING LOVE

CHOOSING LOVE

IN A BROKEN WORLD

HEIDI JOHNSTON

10 Publishing
a division of 10 of those.com

First published in Great Britain in 2019

British Library Cataloguing in Publication Data
A record for this book is available from the British Library

ISBN: 978-1-912373-80-2

Designed by Jude May
Cover image © avean | iStock

Printed in Denmark by Nørhaven

10Publishing, a division of 10ofthose.com
Unit C, Tomlinson Road, Leyland, PR25 2DY, England
Email: info@10ofthose.com
Website: www.10ofthose.com

To Ellie and Lara,
never forget that you are already loved.

I pray that out of his glorious riches he may strengthen you with power through his Spirit in your inner being, so that Christ may dwell in your hearts through faith. And I pray that you, being rooted and established in love, may have power, together with all the Lord's holy people, to grasp how wide and long and high and deep is the love of Christ, and to know this love that surpasses knowledge – that you may be filled to the measure of all the fullness of God.

(Ephesians 3:16–21)

CONTENTS

ACKNOWLEDGEMENTS

IT WOULD BE impossible to list every person who has prayed for me and encouraged me throughout the course of writing this book but I am so grateful for every one of you. It is truly a privilege to be part of God's kingdom.

I would like to give special thanks to: Jonathan Carswell, Lois Ferguson, Julie Hatherall and everyone at 10Publishing, for your enthusiasm, your professionalism and your commitment to telling God's story.

My church family at Scrabo, for teaching me what it means to live as part of a community. In particular, the 'Haverim', without whom I doubt this project would have happened. I will be eternally grateful for you as study partners and some of my most treasured friends.

Everyone at the Rabbit Room, for continually reminding me, in so many beautiful ways, that the stories are true.

Gina and Anne Smith; Helena Sorenson Aman; Lanier Ivester; Sarah Mawhinney; Nicola, Leah and Sarah Foster; Barbara, Hannah and Rebekah McCartney; Rachel, Bethany and Emily Penny; Karin McIlwaine and Robert Hamilton, for your feedback, encouragement and wisdom.

Mum and Dad, for your endless patience and support, for all the drafts you have read and commented on and, perhaps most importantly, for having the courage to live what you believe.

Glenn, for all the repeated conversations, for the encouragement and reassurance and for making me laugh when that was what I needed most. Most of all, thank you for sticking with me through all the ups and downs of the last twenty years. I love you.

Ellie and Lara, thank you for enthusiastically reading all the drafts I gave you and responding with honesty, wisdom and patience. You are remarkable girls and I love you both so much. Whatever the future holds, never stop pursuing the One who loves you most.

Finally, to You, my God and Saviour. May these few faltering words, written in weakness, be used in your strength to push back against the darkness and build your kingdom.

1

DEAR READER…

I'M GLAD YOU **are here. Before we go any further, there's something I want you to know.**

Right now, in this moment, you are already loved.

The greatest love you will ever experience will not be found in another person but in the God who placed the stars in the sky, who brings the sun up every morning, who gave you life and who was prepared to give up everything so you could know him. He loves you endlessly, completely and just as you are. You can do nothing to make him love you more and nothing to make him love you less. No matter what happens in your life, whether you marry or don't, whether you have children or don't, no relationship will ever matter more than your relationship with the God who carries your name on his heart. If you can really grasp that, I have a feeling that the rest of this book will feel like common sense.

If you were hoping for advice on when to date, how to date or even if you should date at all, it's only fair to tell you now that we're going to talk more about love and marriage than we are about dating. I realise that might seem like a strange choice. Surely you need to figure out dating before you start to think about love and marriage? You don't need to think about what might happen in the future until you get there, right?

Think about how often we start preparing for the future long before it happens. If you want to be an Olympic athlete, you start training when you are just a child. If you want to be a great musician, you spend hours and hours practising. Often before you are ready, you start to choose subjects at school that will help you with the career you might be interested in. The person we marry or the decision whether to get married at all will have a huge impact on our lives, yet we do very little to prepare ourselves. To me that doesn't make a lot of sense.

The reason we are not going to focus on dating is simple. It's not because I'm trying to avoid the subject; I know that those conversations are important. It's because I think it makes sense to decide where you are going before you decide how to get there. The kind of love you want to end up with will impact if, when and who you date along the way. My prayer is that, in God's design for relationships, you will catch a glimpse of a love that so many people before you have missed. This love is so beautiful that it is worth working towards.

DEAR READER...

We live in a world where instant happiness seems more important than something better that is further down the road. What is easy often appears more desirable than what is good. If you believe the messages that will come at you from most movies, TV shows and adverts, and maybe even from some of your friends, you will be fooled into settling for love that is just a shadow of the real thing. To live in the twenty-first century and pursue the kind of love God describes in the Bible takes enormous courage.

We're going to look at lots of things together, including why other people matter so much to us, what it actually means to love someone (this one might be a bit surprising!), what you might want to look for in someone you are eventually going to marry and why sex was God's idea all along. Through it all, I hope you will see that God is on your side. He created you, he understands you and he knows what you need even better than you do. The problem is that unless we allow him to teach us how to love and be loved, we will always settle for less. The love God wants for you, even when it takes courage, is better than anything you'll find on your own.

Starting with chapter two, you will notice that each chapter ends with three short sections: *Questions*, *Think about* and *Digging deeper*. You don't have to use these sections but you might find they help you think through what you have read.

Questions

If you will be working through this book with a parent or youth leader, or even a friend, it would be great to discuss these together. (If you are planning to discuss it with a parent, get them to read the letter at the back of the book first.) I know it can take courage to be honest about some of these subjects but if you get used to talking openly now, you'll find it so much easier to talk about any bigger issues that might come up later.

Even if you are reading the book on your own, the discussion questions can be used to help you reflect on each chapter.

Either way, you may also find it helpful as you read each chapter to have a journal handy, where you can write down questions you have, things you have learned or even decisions you have made about your own approach to relationships. These subjects are important and you might want to come back to them again at a later stage.

Think about

Each chapter finishes with the same three questions:

- Was there anything in this chapter that you found difficult to understand? If so, what was it?
- What did you learn from this chapter that you hadn't thought about before?
- Can you think of one question you have after reading this chapter?

These are designed to help you explore anything you have been thinking about that was not covered in the discussion questions.

Digging deeper

If you feel you want to go into the subject of the chapter in more detail, or have questions that haven't been answered, the Bible passages mentioned will give you a place to start.

One last thing: before you start reading, why not pray that God would help you understand the things he is trying to teach you and show you what it looks like to love people the way he does? That's a prayer he is longing to answer!

Let's get started!

2

MADE IN THE IMAGE OF GOD

HAVE YOU EVER noticed how much our lives are affected by the people around us? As babies, we turn instinctively towards the sound of a familiar voice. When we start a new school, the first thing we want to do is find a friend. The kind of home we grow up in and the friendships we develop have a huge impact on the person we become. Whether we like it or not, we are often identified by the people in our lives. At different stages in life we might be known as someone's daughter or someone's sister or someone's wife or someone's mum or even someone's friend, in the same way that those people can be known by their relationship to us. Why is it that the families we are part of and the friends we make have so much power to shape us, for good or bad?

The answer is so important that we have to go back to the very beginning to find it – not just to the beginning of your story or my story but to the beginning of the story of the world itself. Back to the emptiness of a yet-to-be-created world, when nothing existed but God.

Then, God spoke into the darkness.

At his command, darkness was invaded by light and silence was replaced with the roar of oceans. Mountains rose up out of dry ground. Plants and flowers burst into a thousand colours. He spoke again and there was sunshine and moonlight and starry skies. Then came elephants and whales and hummingbirds and tadpoles, called out of nothing simply by the sound of his voice. God looked at what he had made and it was good. Yet, even with all this beauty and colour and life, there was something missing.

God spoke again: 'Let us make mankind in our image' (Genesis 1:26).

Like a potter turning an ordinary piece of clay into a priceless work of art, he took the dust of the earth itself and began to create something very different from what had gone before. Gently, he formed bones and muscles and skin. A heart that could beat and lungs that would fill with air. Arms and legs and fingers and toes. A face with eyes that would see him and a mouth that was ready to smile.

Then, like a kiss of blessing, he bent and breathed his creation into life.

In that moment, filled with the breath of God, mankind was born. Human beings were like God in a way that nothing else in creation could ever be. Deep within them, placed there by God himself, was an ability to think and feel and love in a way that the rest of creation could not.

Like him, they had the ability to create. They could take the gifts that God had given them and turn them into something beautiful. Colour and music and words and rhythm would become paintings and songs and stories and dance. Seeds would be planted and harvested, homes would be built, and children would be taught and nurtured and loved.

Like him they were created to be active. (Notice how often God is described as *doing* something.) He always intended his people to have lives that were full of purpose, working in the world he had made, protecting it and preserving it, and enjoying the good things that he had poured extravagantly into it. He wanted his people to live lives that painted a picture of his heart.

Like him (and this is where the answer to our question begins) they were made for relationships. Did you notice that, when God talked about creating mankind, he said, 'Let *us* make mankind in *our* image' (my italics)? You see, before there were people, God already existed in a relationship. Somehow, before the beginning of time, in a way we find impossible to fully understand, God the Father, God the Son and God the Holy Spirit were already there. They were all involved in the creation of the world, they each depended on each other and they were *all God*.

If you find that confusing, you are not alone. I do too! In fact, it's been baffling even the smartest people since the beginning of time. Whether we understand it or not, the important thing is that it tells us something about God. We were made by a God who knows what it is to love. Actually, the Bible tells us that God doesn't just *understand* love; he *is* love.

The fact that relationships have always been at the heart of God explains why they matter so much to us. We were never created to journey through life alone. We were made to live in families and communities, to have friends and neighbours. When God looked at the very first man, he knew immediately that it was not good for him to be alone. It just didn't work. From the very beginning, people have needed other people.

The problems began when the same people who had walked with God in the Garden of Eden chose to set aside his design for life and make up their own rules. The beautiful reflection of God that had once burned so brightly was pushed down and buried under a mountain of bad choices and broken hearts. Without him, something broke inside them and that changed everything, even the way they looked at each other.

The bad news is that every single relationship, whether it is between parents and children, between husbands and wives or in friendships, has been affected by our decision to do things our own way. Even though we need each other as much as ever, we have forgotten how to love like he does.

The brokenness inside every one of us means relationships that were designed for our good can actually cause us pain.

Sometimes families break up, friends hurt each other and husbands and wives go back on the promises they made. Too often we are selfish and careless with other people's hearts. It's not because relationships are a bad idea; it's because we are broken people in a broken world and we have turned love into something so much smaller than it was meant to be.

The good news is that God hasn't given up on us. When Adam and Eve left the Garden of Eden, God already knew what it would take to make everything right. Because of Jesus' death on the cross it is possible to walk with God again. One day he will make everything perfect but for now he walks with us in the beautiful, painful, wonderful adventure of ordinary life. Whether we are hopeful, scared, excited, confused or even sad, when we come to him and choose to listen to his voice, he has a way of taking broken things and making them beautiful.

Questions

- Read Genesis 1:26–27. What does it mean to be made in the image of God? In what ways do we reflect his character? Why are relationships so important to us? In what ways does the sin that started with Adam and Eve make relationships more difficult?
- What are some of the ways that our selfishness can affect our relationships with the people we love?

Think about

- Was there anything in this chapter that you found difficult to understand? If so, what was it?
- What did you learn from this chapter that you hadn't thought about before?
- Can you think of one question you have after reading this chapter?

Digging deeper

- Genesis 2–3 (God creates Adam and Eve).
- Ephesians 2:10 (God has created us with a purpose).

3

WHY RELATIONSHIPS?

IN A WORLD of more than seven billion people it is truly amazing to know that God is interested in us individually. He knows you and loves you, and has a plan for your life. The choices you make matter enormously to him, including who you fall in love with and who you eventually marry (or if you end up getting married at all). Since romantic relationships are the main subject of this book, I'm tempted to dive in and start talking about them right now. I promise we'll get there soon but first, in the next couple of chapters, there are some important things I'd like you to think about.

In the last chapter we talked about the idea that, as people made in the image of God, we were created to live in relationship with God and with each other. When we are welcomed into God's family, we become part of something bigger than we could ever imagine. While it's absolutely true that our choices matter to God, sometimes we can be so focused on his individual plan for us that we forget we are part of the epic story God began writing before the creation of the world. Before we can understand what it means to live in a deep, unique relationship with one specific person, first we need to learn to see our lives as part of God's incredible story.

Have you ever noticed how many great books and movies involve a band of characters learning to work together to accomplish something that changes the world they live in? I wonder if it's because that story is part of who we were created to be, in a way we often miss. You might be surprised to discover that the lives we live together and the way we treat one another are right at the heart of sharing God's love with the world. We can't fully live the life that he has called us to without understanding how to love the people in our lives.

God has given his people the task of telling the story of his incredible, unending, unbreakable love for the world. At the centre is Jesus, coming to earth as a man and dying in our place so that we can know God and live in relationship with him again forever. God's story is so enormous and wonderful and breathtakingly, impossibly, completely true that it will take all of us working together to tell it well. This is a story that can't just be told in words; it's also a picture that is painted by the lives we live and the way we choose to love.

After the Garden of Eden, it didn't take long for people to forget about God. In order to remind them who he was and how much he loved them, God chose a man called Abraham to be part of his great rescue plan. He promised that one day he would give Abraham's family (who later became known as the Israelites) a country of their own, where they could live as his people and get to know him together. As they learned how to follow him, listening to him and obeying his voice, they would become a living picture of what God was like.

Even before they had set foot in their new country, God reminded his people how important it was to follow him *together*.

First, by living in obedience to God, they would be constantly teaching each other what it meant to belong to him. They would remind each other that they were treasured, loved and precious to God, and that his plans for them were always good. They would remind each other that God had never broken his promises and that, one day, he was going to do something truly incredible to fix the problem of their wandering hearts. They would remind each other not to forget him again.

Second, if they obeyed God together, the lives they lived and the way they treated each other would allow the world to catch a glimpse of the character of God. When the Israelites looked after each other and showed kindness, the people watching would see a God whose heart was full of love. When they took sin seriously and were careful about the way they worshipped God, his holiness would shine through. When they forgave each other, their neighbours would begin to realise that God's people could only forgive because God had first forgiven them. Through the loving lives of his people, the dim, long-buried memories of God that were hidden in the hearts of those watching on would begin to stir and lead them home to him.

Again and again throughout the Bible the same plan keeps showing up, as God invites his people to use their lives and their love to tell his story together.

If loving each other was always part of God's plan for his people, it shouldn't surprise us that Jesus spent a lot of time talking about it. Speaking to his followers, he said, 'By this everyone will know that you are my disciples, if you love one another' (John 13:35). According to Jesus, loving each other is one of the most important ways we can show that we love God and belong to him. In the same way, not loving other people suggests that we don't love God. That's how important it is.

We see how much our love for each other mattered to Jesus on the night he was arrested and taken to be crucified. In the midst of his grief and pain, he took time to pray for the people who would one day trust in him. (If you are following him, that includes you.) He prayed that we would love each other deeply, with the same incredible, selfless, unbreakable love that existed between Jesus and his Father before the beginning of time.

Jesus knew that if we let him teach us and give us the strength to love like that, our love would be proof to the world that the story we are telling is true. He also knew that when we tear each other down with cruel words and unkind behaviour, the people watching might well decide that the story itself is a lie. I don't think that's something we take seriously enough.

Let's be honest, love isn't always easy. If you read the story of the Israelites, you'll see that they messed up again and again, forgetting who they truly were and fighting against each other. There will always be people in our schools and colleges, our towns, our churches and even in our families that we find it hard to love. We are all different. Often those differences, combined with the fact that we are still broken and selfish on the inside, make it hard to get along. Yet, according to Jesus, if we really love God and want to live as part of his family, loving each other is not optional.

In the book of Ephesians, Paul is writing to a church that was struggling to figure out how to love each other in the way God was asking. They came from different backgrounds, were good at different things, had different personalities and wanted to worship God in different ways. Interestingly, instead of these differences being a problem to overcome, Paul says that some were gifts from God to help them stand strong and tell the story together.

Paul tells the Ephesians (just as Moses had told the Israelites) that following God *together* will help them know God better and love him more. If they understand that their gifts and talents have been given for the good of others, they will use them to make the church stronger. Instead of being like a little boat tossed on a stormy sea, changing direction and getting battered by every strong wind, they will be able to stand firm. Growing together in their understanding of

God and their love for one another, the story they tell will shine brightly, piercing the darkness of a broken world and pointing it to God.

Within each of us God has placed unique personalities, gifts and talents that allow us to reflect his heart in a million different ways. Imagine a giant jigsaw with countless tiny pieces. Each piece on its own has a specific shape and colour and pattern, but it's only when all the pieces fit together that you get to see the big picture. God may have called you to tell his story in your own small way but when you offer your life, talents and abilities to tell the bigger story, the world sees a clearer picture of our breathtaking God. If each of us focuses on our own little story, refusing to love one another and tell God's story together, the picture is incomplete. The pieces are there but it has never become the complete masterpiece it was created to be.

That's why, before we think about romantic relationships, you need to understand why love in general is so important. The way we treat the people in our lives matters more than we can possibly imagine. If that is true for those we live beside, or those we go to church with, or our friends and families, can you imagine how much it matters when it comes to loving the person we choose to spend our lives with?

Questions

- Can you think of how a gift or talent you have, or even your unique personality, could be used for the good of other people or the telling of God's story?

- Read 1 John 4:19–21. What do you learn from these verses about loving one another?
- If we are Christians, how might the way we treat others affect other people's view of God? How seriously do you take this?
- Why do you think we need to understand the importance of loving others before we think about the idea of romantic relationships?

Think about

- Was there anything in this chapter that you found difficult to understand? If so, what was it?
- What did you learn from this chapter that you hadn't thought about before?
- Can you think of one question you have after reading this chapter?

Digging deeper

- Genesis 12:1–3 and 17:1–8 (God calls Abraham).
- John 17:20–26 (Jesus prays for believers before he is arrested).
- 1 Peter 2:9 (we are called to tell God's story together).
- Ephesians 4:1–6 and 11–16 (we need to be united).
- Luke 6:35 (we should love our enemies).

4

WHAT IS LOVE?

IN THE LAST chapter we discovered that loving one another is right at the heart of living in God's story and sharing it with the world around us. There is an important question we didn't ask: 'What does it actually mean to love someone?'

Often, when people talk about love, they are referring to the feelings they have towards someone. You may have noticed that different relationships come with different emotions. The way you feel about your family is probably not the same as the way you feel about your friends. When it comes to romantic love, the feelings can be overwhelming. Just being in the same room as the other person can leave you with a racing heart, sweaty hands and a sudden inability to think clearly or speak in proper sentences.

God intentionally designed us as people with feelings. I'm glad he did. I can't imagine a world where I was able to look at a beautiful sunset without feeling wonder; or hold the hand of someone I love and not feel a warm rush of pleasure; or hold my tiny, newborn daughter for the first time and not feel like my heart might burst; or stand beside the grave of my friend and not feel broken and sad inside.

Feeling things deeply is part of being human. On the other hand, if love is *only* something that we feel, we are left with some major problems.

First, what do we do when we know God has commanded us to love someone but we just don't feel that way? There are always going to be people towards whom we don't feel love. It's hard to feel much love for a stranger whose life doesn't really impact our own. Sometimes the people we do know can be so different from us that we struggle to easily understand them or find common ground. There may be people in our lives who have hurt us in ways we find hard to forgive. If you have ever tried to force yourself to feel something that doesn't come naturally, you'll know how hard it is.

Second, even with people we naturally love, our feelings can come and go. Tiredness or stress or hormones have a habit of stepping in and messing with our emotions. Changing circumstances or just getting older can affect how we feel in unexpected ways. Even the most dramatic and intense romantic feelings towards a person can (and almost certainly will) change or fade over time.

The third problem with feelings is that they can be unreliable. Let me tell you a story that might help to explain what I mean by this.When I was growing up, my Grandpa loved to sail. He and his friends would head out on his boat, then come home with all sorts of stories about their adventures. On one particular day they had travelled to Scotland and then, as usual, used the boat's compass to plot their journey back home to Belfast. What they didn't realise was that someone had set a magnet beside the compass. That was a really bad idea. Instead of pointing exactly north, the compass had been pulled off course and was guiding them in the wrong direction. You can imagine their dismay when it became clear that they were lost in the middle of the Irish Sea, with no idea how to get back home. The danger with relying completely on how we feel is that we won't notice when our feelings are pulling us in the wrong direction. In chapter two we discovered that the choice we made to forget God and go our own way has affected every part of us, turning our understanding of love upside down. In some ways it's a little like the magnet that was set down beside my Grandpa's compass. When we follow the advice to 'trust our feelings' or 'follow our heart', we often end up somewhere we never intended to go, wondering how on earth we got there. Instead of thinking first about God and then each other, our thoughts tend to go immediately to what we think will make us most happy. When it comes to loving God and loving others, this instinct to put ourselves first is a big problem.

What do we do when our feelings let us down? What happens in the moments when those feelings simply aren't there? If they change or disappear completely, does that mean love becomes impossible? How can we know if our feelings are pointing us in the wrong direction?

The good news is that God does not expect us to live in a constant state of warm, fuzzy affection for each other. (It's ok to be relieved about that!) He made us and he knows exactly what our hearts are like. While what we feel can be thrilling and wonderful, the love that God has called us to live out is so great and beautiful that even the strongest feelings will not be enough to make it possible. When he commands us to love one another, he is not asking us to try and whip up a feeling of love. He is asking us, with his help, to learn to love in a way that puts our emotions in their proper place. Because he created us, loves us and knows what will satisfy us, he wants to teach us a whole new way of loving.

Real love is not just a response in your heart or in your stomach; it is also a decision in your mind that is bigger than what you feel at a particular moment in time. That might sound surprising but I hope you are beginning to see why it could be very good news.

Do you remember Jesus' words in John 13:35, when he reminds his disciples that loving each other is proof of their love for him? Right before that, in verse 34, he tells them the secret of this new kind of love: 'A new command I give you: love one another. As I have loved you, so you must love one another.' According to Jesus, love means intentionally choosing to treat people the same way that he did.

Have you ever really paid attention to the way Jesus loved people? In a world that tells us to put ourselves first his love is astonishing.

One day, exhausted and hungry, Jesus and his disciples set out in a boat to find a quiet place to rest and eat. When they arrived at the shore, they discovered that a huge crowd of people were already waiting. Despite his tiredness and hunger, Jesus looked at the crowd and loved them. Instead of sending them away, he took the time to teach and feed them, putting their needs above his own (Mark 6:30–44).

On another long, hot, tiring journey Jesus chose to walk even further so that he could help a woman who had been rejected by her entire town because of the mistakes she had made (John 4:3–29).

When you are reading the stories of Jesus' life, look out for how he dealt with people: listening to them; spending time with them; feeding them when they were hungry; healing them when they were hurting or sick. Again and again his love was demonstrated by his actions. In Paul's letter to the Ephesians (the same one we looked at in chapter three), he reminds them that real love means following Jesus' example: showing kindness and compassion; having patience with each other; forgiving one another the way God forgives us. Love means putting the other person first, whether we feel like it or not.

Instead of thinking, 'How can this person make me happy?' real love turns our broken instincts the right way up and asks, 'What can I do to love this person like Jesus?' Sometimes it might mean staying quiet when you are tempted to share a piece of gossip, or standing up for someone when it would be easier to say nothing. When your friend is in a bad mood and speaks to you harshly, loving them like Jesus may mean doing something to help them instead of fighting back. At home it could mean offering to do the dishes, even though you are tired. It might even mean letting go of something you are angry about, whether the other person deserves your forgiveness or not.

You may have noticed how often Jesus spent time with people who had messed up and were looked down on by others. He saw the worst things they had thought and said and done, even when they couldn't see it themselves, and he loved them anyway. His love was never based on whether the person deserved it. Given that he was completely holy and sinless, you might expect that people who were sinful and broken would want to avoid Jesus. Instead, when they saw his love, they followed him everywhere he went. The beautiful thing about Jesus was not just that he loved people as they were. Knowing they would only ever be satisfied by a relationship with the God who loved them, he told the truth about their brokenness and reminded them that they were created for more.

Jesus' love didn't stop at caring for people or showing them kindness. The greatest act of love that has ever been, or ever will be, happened when Jesus chose to die on a cross. He took the place of people who had turned their backs on him and gave up his life for them, even when they hated him. As the Son of God, with one word he could have ended the pain and suffering and humiliation of the cross. Instead, because of his love for us, he chose to stay there alone, naked and in agony. He took the punishment we deserved and opened up a way for us to once again live the lives for which we were created. There are no words big enough to describe a love like that.

If anyone understood what real love looks like and how difficult it is, the apostle John did. As one of Jesus' closest friends, John spent more time with him than almost anyone. He knew what it felt like to be loved by Jesus and he had watched Jesus show love to others. He stood at the cross and watched what Jesus suffered for the people he loved. He understood that the kind of love Jesus showed is only possible when it comes from God himself. Looking back on all he had learned from Jesus, John says, 'We love because he first loved us' (1 John 4:19).

One of the many wonderful things about God is that he never asks us to do something without giving us everything we need to do it. He knows that even when we want to love like Jesus, the brokenness in our hearts means we can't do it alone. Way back in the book of Ezekiel, when the Israelites were struggling and failing to love the way God had asked them to, he promised his people that it wouldn't always be like this. In Ezekiel 36:26 God made this promise: 'I will give you a new heart and put a new spirit in you.' When we come to Jesus and give our lives to him, accepting the forgiveness that he offers through the cross, the Holy Spirit comes to live within us. Then, when we walk with him and listen to his voice, he helps us to love in ways that we could never manage on our own. That's one of the reasons why loving others like Jesus is proof that we belong to him.

It could be that when you imagine setting aside your own feelings and choosing instead to love in this way, you picture yourself ending up miserable or bored. If you are anything like me, it's probably more appealing to take the easy option – to go with what feels good and hope for the best. You might be tempted to believe that putting yourself first is the way to find happiness. When we believe this is true, we forget that God is generous and good and that he always wants the best for us. If he asks us to make hard choices, it's because he can see the bigger picture. He wants us to have something better than we would discover on our own. That's true when it comes to loving the people around us and it is also true with romantic love.

When we keep choosing love, whether we feel like it or not, something amazing often happens. In the process of loving intentionally, our feelings begin to change. In the end, we find ourselves overwhelmed by love that is deeper and more real than we ever expected.

Questions

- Why does relying completely on our feelings make it so hard to love like Jesus?
- What difference could it make in a relationship if love is a choice and not just a feeling?

- Why might you need God's help to choose to act in a way that shows love? How might that look in a family relationship? With your friends? In a romantic relationship?
- Read 1 Corinthians 13:1–7. According to these verses, what is real love like? What might that look like in everyday life?

Think about

- Was there anything in this chapter that you found difficult to understand? If so, what was it?
- What did you learn from this chapter that you hadn't thought about before?
- Can you think of one question you have after reading this chapter?

Digging deeper

- John 13:34–35 and 15:12–17 (Jesus urges us to love one another).
- 1 John 4:7–21 (if we love God, we will love one another).
- Mark 12:28–33 (love is the most important commandment).
- Romans 12:10 (we are to put others first).

5

SHARING THE ADVENTURE

SO FAR WE have talked a lot about the fact that God created us to live in relationship with others. It's clear that the way we love the people in our lives matters.

For the rest of this book we are going to focus on the one particular kind of love that seems to captivate us more than any other. It's the subject of most of our popular songs and it crops up to some degree in most of the stories in our books and movies.

Sometimes, without realising it, I think we almost believe that the whole idea of romantic love came from Hollywood. The truth is that even the greatest movies, books and songs are just an echo of something that is older, deeper and more real than anything we could write or imagine.

You may have noticed that many of the Hollywood romances share one thing in common: they end in the same place. Very often the girl and boy meet and have an instant attraction to each other. Typically some kind of obstacle keeps them apart but then, against all odds, they finally get together. The movie finishes with a dramatic kiss (or more), a declaration of love or occasionally even a wedding. The problem with the Hollywood ending is that it suggests the story is over. The romance and excitement has reached its conclusion and nothing that comes afterwards is considered interesting enough to be included in a movie.

There is no doubt that the early stages of a relationship are exciting. Towards the end of my time at university, I remember coming home on a break to the town where my family had just bought a house. I couldn't help noticing the red-haired guy with the infectious smile who was one of the youth leaders at their new church. Not long after I moved back home, I bumped into him in a shop. In a move I now know was completely out of character, he asked me if I'd like to go out for dinner. That first evening was a little strained at times (we hardly knew each other and we were both trying pretty hard to be impressive) but there was something about him that captivated me. For a while I struggled to concentrate on anything else. I spent hours replaying our conversations in my mind. I had butterflies in my stomach on a Friday night, knowing I would see him over the weekend. If our romance had been a Hollywood movie, it probably would have ended a few months later when we sat under the stars and finally declared our love for each other.

Can I let you into a secret? Wonderful as it was, that wasn't even close to being the best bit. If the story ended there, we would have missed something deeper and richer that has grown through years of sharing both the adventure and the difficulties of life. I still keep the petals of the rose he gave me on our first date but I wouldn't trade what we have now for the excitement of those early days.

In order to understand real, deep romantic love that grows with the passing of time, instead of just the excitement of falling in love, we need to go back to Genesis again to see where it all started.

Genesis 2 tells us that after God created Adam, forming him with his own hands and breathing him into life, he planted a beautiful garden and placed Adam in it. When I read about the Garden of Eden, for a long time I imagined something between the pictures in children's story Bibles and the garden behind my house. However, a careful examination of the description in Genesis 2:8–15 shows the image in my mind was much too small. Rather than a patch of ground with some bushes, fruit trees and a few friendly animals, the Garden of Eden was more like a vast national park. It included four rivers; countless different trees; gold and precious stones; animals of every size and kind imaginable; and an abundance of food that would make your mouth water.

I'll never forget the day I was taken to Grandview in West Virginia. My family and I were staying with some good friends when one day, after lunch, they invited us to go for a walk. Talking and laughing, we climbed a forest trail through some trees and came out into a clearing. I was completely unprepared for what I saw. The hillside fell away into a vast canyon, covered on both sides by a thick blanket of trees. At the bottom of the canyon was a river that wound its way around the land on the other side, creating what looked like a magical island. The sheer beauty of it was overwhelming.

As an eagle flew past, I remember standing in stunned silence, thinking, 'God didn't have to make it this beautiful. We don't need this to survive. This is kindness on a level I can't understand.' I don't know what the Garden of Eden looked like or how Adam felt the first time he saw it but, if the majesty of Grandview can exist in our broken world, then the perfect, unspoilt beauty of that garden must have been indescribable.

In his abundant kindness, God not only gave Adam food that would make his body strong and beauty that would make his soul sing; he also gave him work that would bring him satisfaction. Like a park ranger, Adam was invited to use his skills and creativity to work alongside God, caring for the incredible home he had been given in a way that would protect and even enhance its beauty.

Yet just as telling God's story to the world requires his people to work together, God had never intended that Adam would undertake this task alone. Even as Adam looked at all the animals and began to realise how different he was from them, God was preparing him for a partner who would be able to share his life in a unique and beautiful way. Genesis 2:21–25 tells the story of what happened next:

> *So the Lord God caused the man to fall into a deep sleep; and while he was sleeping, he took one of the man's ribs and then closed up the place with flesh. Then the Lord God made a woman from the rib he had taken out of the man, and he brought her to the man. The man said,*
>
> *'This is now bone of my bones*
> *and flesh of my flesh;*
> *she shall be called "woman",*
> *for she was taken out of man.'*
>
> *That is why a man leaves his father and mother and is united to his wife, and they become one flesh.*
> *Adam and his wife were both naked, and they felt no shame.*

When Adam opened his eyes and saw the woman God had made, he was astonished. Like Adam, she was created in the image of God (who loved them equally), reflecting God's character in many of the same ways that made Adam uniquely human. At the same time, she was so distinctly different that Adam could hardly tear his eyes away from her. Two halves of the same whole, God had designed Adam and Eve to fit together, not just physically but emotionally and spiritually, in a way that was remarkable.

When verse 25 states that Adam and Eve were naked and felt no shame, it is about much more than the fact that they weren't wearing any clothes. The bond between them was so close that they had nothing to hide. There were no secrets, no shame and no fear of being seen for who they really were. In the presence of God they were free to love each other fully. Not only could they know each other intimately and deeply, they could enjoy an unbroken, intimate, relationship with God himself, walking with him and working alongside him as they cared for his creation together.

I don't have particularly good co-ordination (I have been known to trip over my own feet) but I do find dancers fascinating. When two ballet dancers move across the floor, spinning and lifting and catching, moving away and coming back together in time with the music, it's stunning to watch. In some mysterious way, it's as if the dancers and the music all become one. I wonder if that's what it was like as Adam and Eve learned to share the beauty of the life they had been given, with bodies and souls working in perfect harmony with God and with each other.

We know that the perfection Adam and Eve experienced didn't last forever. One of the immediate consequences of their choice to disobey God was that, for the first time, they noticed they were naked. As innocence disappeared, doubt, suspicion and fear crept in and began to change the way they looked at each other.

God knew before he created Adam and Eve that they would one day have to leave the garden. He knew that their love, and every love from that point on, would be touched by grief and sadness as well as joy. He knew the desire to fight for their own interests would threaten the perfect harmony they had enjoyed in the garden. He also knew that, despite everything they faced, they would need each other more than ever.

The fact that we are broken people in a broken world often affects the way we relate to each other but it doesn't change the beauty of the special relationship God created. Partnership like the one between Adam and Eve has always been part of God's plan. It was necessary and beautiful in the perfection of the Garden of Eden, and it was necessary and beautiful in the brokenness that came later.

Sometimes we get so caught up in arguments about the differences between men and women that we forget those differences are part of God's design. When we read in Genesis 2:18 that Eve was created as a helper suitable for Adam, it is easy to misunderstand what that means, as if Eve was a lesser character in the story. I almost hesitate to mention the word 'helper' for fear of the images it conjures up for some people. The problem is that if we ignore it, we miss so much of the beauty and genius of God's design for relationships.

In fact, the same word 'helper' is also used repeatedly to describe the help God brings to his people. In Deuteronomy 33:26 Moses reminds the Israelites that God is unique, powerful and completely trustworthy with this description: '[God] rides across the heavens to help you and on the clouds in his majesty.' In verse 29 he describes God as 'your shield and helper'. The writer of Psalm 121:1–2 says,

I lift up my eyes to the mountains –
where does my help come from?
My help comes from the L*ORD*,
the Maker of heaven and earth.

In these verses, God is not just giving a little extra assistance, as some might understand the word helper. He is coming alongside his people and offering them his strength when they are overwhelmed by a situation they can't handle alone.

One of the great mysteries of romantic love is the way two completely different people can come together, combining to form a new unit, complementing each other and working in harmony in a way that shapes them both. Like fellow soldiers in an epic battle, when they learn to work together, their differences make them stronger together than they are apart. Together they are able to fulfil the task God has given them in a way that neither could do alone.

So often we miss the fact that romantic love and marriage were not just created for the purpose of satisfying each other but for journeying together in the same direction and helping each other towards the same goal. Adam and Eve were not only designed to provide each other with companionship and pleasure; they were perfectly matched and dependant on one another in the important work to which God had called them.

Just as it does in any relationship, real love within a romantic relationship means putting the other person first, whether you feel like it or not. That's why we first had to consider what it means to love at all. Romantic love may be deep and intimate in a different way but heightened emotions don't change the fact that love is a choice as well as a feeling.

Like any love, romantic love is best expressed in actions. It is demonstrated in the way we choose to treat each other and the way we care for one another. We show it in the way we speak to each other and the way we speak about each other, both in public and in private.

Love, as God intended, also has a unique goal: it always encourages the other person to know and love him more deeply. As a husband and wife grow to be more like Jesus, walking with him and living out his love, the bond that is forged between them becomes a clearer picture of the heart of God.

Whatever God specifically calls us to do, there is a grand adventure in ordinary life that many people miss. Whether we are sharing the important job of raising families to know and love him, living as part of a community or using a unique skill to heal or teach or bring order, God still calls us to partner with each other and with him in the work of restoring our broken world and demonstrating his love to the people around us.

Questions

- What difference will it make if a husband and wife are working together to serve God, rather than focusing only on making each other happy?

- How important is it that a husband and wife encourage each other to get to know God better? How might that happen in everyday life?
- If part of love is working together to serve God, what difference will that make when it comes to choosing who you will marry?

Think about

- Was there anything in this chapter that you found difficult to understand? If so, what was it?
- What did you learn from this chapter that you hadn't thought about before?
- Can you think of one question you have after reading this chapter?

Digging deeper

- Genesis 2:18–25 (God creates Eve).
- Acts 18:1–3, 18–19, 24–26 (Priscilla and her husband, Aquilla, serve God together).

6

THE UNBREAKABLE PROMISE

IN *The Green Ember* adventure series, two young rabbits find themselves drawn into an epic quest that changes their lives forever. As they begin to forge deep friendships with other rabbits, standing shoulder to shoulder to fight for the true home they will one day share, the rabbits learn an old promise. Even before I read the book, the words of the oath they swear to each other captured my imagination:

My place beside you, my blood for yours.
Till the Green Ember rises, or the end of the world.[1]

In a world where promises can be made lightly and broken easily, loyalty like this might seem to belong only in fairy tales. The longing it stirs within us to be part of something bigger than ourselves – loving and being loved without any fear of abandonment or rejection – feels like an impossible wish. Like the dream of living in a castle made of chocolate or inventing a time machine, it's crazy and wonderful but appears to have nothing to do with real life. If that's how you feel, I can't wait to tell you about covenants.

A covenant is a binding agreement, a bit like a contract or a promise, only more serious, more beautiful and intended to be broken only by death. In Bible times they were a familiar part of life. Friends made covenants with each other, promising to look after and protect each other for the rest of their lives. Sometimes two groups or countries would make a covenant of peace, vowing not to attack each other and promising to help if the other came under attack from someone else. Amazingly, there are also times in the Bible when God himself chooses to make covenants with the people he loves.

In order to really understand the commitment behind God's design for marriage, we have to discover the importance of these covenants in the Bible. One of my favourite things about the Bible is the way God tells stories and creates pictures in our minds, capturing our imaginations and helping us understand the importance of ideas that are too big for words alone. Since covenants were permanent promises that would change the relationship between the people involved forever, they were usually made during a ceremony full of signs and symbols you could see, touch and even taste. This not only helped people understand the seriousness of what was taking place but also created lasting reminders of the promises that had been made. While it can be a little difficult to get your head around some of the details of covenant ceremonies, particularly as our culture is so different from that of Bible times, the pictures they paint are beautiful.

As oaths were sworn, those involved would call on God as the witness of the covenant, recognising that he would be the Judge of anyone who broke it. Sometimes pieces of clothing or weapons would be exchanged as symbols of the unbreakable promise that had passed between the friends and the bond of loyalty that would continue for the rest of their lives.

In a culture where eating together was taken much more seriously than it is now, inviting someone to share a meal was a declaration of friendship and peace. As a result, covenant ceremonies often ended with the sharing of a covenant meal.

One aspect of covenant ceremonies that can be difficult to understand is the importance of blood (although the idea of becoming blood brothers is still common in some cultures). The wine shared during the covenant meal was often seen as a symbol of the blood of those people involved and the fact that their lives were now joined – as though their blood actually ran in each other's veins. The covenant ceremony often also involved the sacrifice of an animal. While this sounds a bit odd and might even make us uncomfortable, it's important to remember how the shedding of the animal's blood was understood back then: as a way of saying nothing but death would release the people involved from the promises they were making.

Not every covenant ceremony involved all of these signs or symbols. However, in every case the making of a covenant was a serious, permanent commitment to stand with the other person, offering everything you had for their care and protection, whatever the cost to you.

If you know the story of David and Jonathan, you may have read about a covenant without realising it. David and Jonathan were close friends who cared deeply about each other. The problem was that Jonathan's father (King Saul) was incredibly jealous of David and wanted to kill him. In 1 Samuel 18:3–4 we read, 'Jonathan made a covenant with David because he loved him as himself. Jonathan took off the robe he was wearing and gave it to David, along with his tunic, and even his sword, his bow and his belt.' Later, when Saul did try to kill David, the covenant relationship between the friends meant that Jonathan willingly put his own life at risk to protect David, helping him find a way to escape from his father.

Earlier in this chapter I mentioned that God also makes covenants with his people. Each one of these covenants is fascinating to read, giving us glimpses of the heart of a God who is faithful and kind, and stops at nothing to demonstrate his love. For now we're going to look briefly at two of the covenants he made.

As an old man with no children or home of his own, Abraham was astonished by God's promise to him: a family that would eventually grow so big it couldn't be counted, and a special relationship with God that would impact the whole world. Abraham believed God and trusted what he said, yet when God went on to promise Abraham's family a land of their own, he asked, 'how can I know?' (Genesis 15:8).

God responded by making the beautiful covenant we read about in Genesis 15. In preparation for the ceremony God told Abraham to kill specific animals and cut them in half, laying the halves out on the ground with a space between them that would form a path. As thick darkness came down and Abraham went into a deep sleep, God walked the path between the animals. In a vivid and stunning picture that Abraham could understand and remember, God was saying that he would die, just as the animals had, before he would break his promises.

God was making it clear, in a dramatic and visual way, that the covenant didn't depend on Abraham. It couldn't be broken by Abraham's failures and it wouldn't be changed by circumstances. Even though God warned Abraham that there would be difficult times in the years to come, he would never need to doubt God's unbreakable promises. No matter what happened, the covenant was utterly trustworthy.

Of all the covenants ever made, one stands out above the others. As Jesus willingly gave up his life on a cross outside Jerusalem, he made a covenant that changed our relationship with God forever. This time there were no animals involved. The blood that ran on to the ground was his. When Jesus died for us, he was offering us a life that would never end and a bond with him that would never be broken. When we choose to give our lives to Jesus, we become his covenant partners and so all that belongs to Jesus is shared with us. Because Jesus has defeated death, we never have to fear it again. Because he will live forever, we will live forever. Because he can come into the presence of God, so can we.

The wonder of this covenant doesn't finish there. Articles of clothing are exchanged as we hand over our ragged attempts to live life on our own terms, trading them for the robes of perfect, sinless righteousness that rightfully belong to Jesus. We can't earn these robes and we will never deserve them but we get to keep them forever. Because of the cross, when God looks at us – no matter what we have done or how we have failed him – he sees the perfection of Jesus, our covenant brother.

When we take communion, we are sharing a covenant meal. This not only reminds us that we have peace with God, but also that we have peace with the others who have been welcomed at his table.

God has made an unbreakable, unending covenant that binds us to him forever, making us his in a way that will never be changed by circumstance or failure. If you can really grasp that, it will change the way you read the Bible and shape the way you understand your relationship with God and with others.

You may wonder how all this is relevant to a book about relationships. We need to understand the importance of covenants because, in God's eyes, marriage is a covenant. If you have been to a wedding, some of the covenant details we have talked about in this chapter may be familiar. When the couple stand up in front of family and friends – acknowledging that they are in the presence of God – they make vows to each other, promising to be faithful until they are separated by death. As they join hands, it is a symbol of the fact that their lives have now become one. The couple also exchange rings as symbols of the covenant they have made. From that point on, these rings will be a reminder – to themselves and others – that they have made promises to be loyal to their husband or wife for the rest of their life.

After the wedding, the bride and groom usually share a meal with their friends and family, celebrating the marriage relationship that now exists between the couple. Later the marriage is sealed in private as the man and woman join their bodies physically (we'll talk more about this in the next chapter!) in a way that beautifully completes the act of becoming one.

Marriage is a gift from the God who created us and knows the design of our hearts. However, as a covenant, it comes with responsibilities that cannot be ignored. Sometimes we can be tempted to take the truth of God's love and forgiveness and twist it to mean that he doesn't mind what we do as long as we feel happy. That is just not true. His commitment to the covenant of marriage has not changed. According to Ephesians 5:32, the unique relationship between a husband and wife is a picture of the covenant love between Jesus and his people. We are called to love one another with the same daring, committed love that Sally Lloyd-Jones so beautifully calls God's 'Never Stopping, Never Giving Up, Unbreaking, Always and Forever Love'.[2]

I write this knowing that some of the people I love have experienced the pain of broken covenants first-hand. Some have had to watch helplessly as the person they love walked away from the covenant they made. Others are living with the fact that they were the one to end a marriage. Some have struggled with the break-up of their parents' marriage.

We have a God who is not only holy but sees our tears and is present in our struggles. He cares about our pain and has the power to bring healing into the most difficult of situations. In his grace, he walks with us through the often painful reality of our broken world, offering comfort to those who have been hurt or betrayed, and forgiveness to those who come to him with their broken promises. Yet, in his holiness and love, he makes it clear that covenants cannot be made and set aside without serious consequences. If we belong to him, the covenant he made with us at the cross means he will never stop loving us, never turn his back on us and never give up on us. That is the example he calls us to follow.

Questions

- Were there any parts of the covenant ceremonies in the Bible that helped you better understand what is happening during and after a wedding? If so, what were they?

- When a covenant is made, how does it change the relationship between the people involved?
- How does the idea of covenant help you understand the commitment of marriage?
- If we have become covenant partners with Jesus because of the cross, how does that help us understand our relationship with him and with God?

Think about

- Was there anything in this chapter that you found difficult to understand? If so, what was it?
- What did you learn from this chapter that you hadn't thought about before?
- Can you think of one question you have after reading this chapter?

Digging deeper

- Genesis 15 (God's covenant with Abraham).
- Jeremiah 31:31–33 and 32:40 (God promises he will make a new covenant).
- Matthew 26:27–28 and Luke 22:19–20 (Jesus talks about his blood making a covenant).
- Malachi 2:14 (marriage is a covenant).

7

THE TRUTH ABOUT SEX

I DON'T KNOW how you feel as you come to a chapter on sex. Maybe it's the chapter you have been waiting for, or maybe the thought of it fills you with horror and you'd really rather skip it. Perhaps you are most worried about the discussion questions at the end. Most likely, you feel a mixture of all three.

In a world that seems to be obsessed with sex and sexuality, it can be difficult to figure out what is true. As we consider where sex fits into God's design for life, we are going to think about five myths that we come across again and again.

I grew up listening to the myth of Finn McCool – the Irish giant who is said to have placed the enormous hexagonal stones that make up the Giant's Causeway on the coast of Northern Ireland. That's not the type of myth I mean. I am talking about a lie that is generally believed to be true, and is repeated so often and so convincingly that we can easily be fooled into accepting it as fact.

As we clear away the myths and discover the true beauty of sex as God intended it, my prayer is not only that you will learn to see it as a good gift from a generous God, but also that you will begin to understand how important it is to handle such a powerful gift wisely.

Myth 1: God disapproves of sex

The first thing you need to know is that sex was God's idea in the first place.

When we see the way it is often misused and the damage it has caused in our broken world, we can sometimes react by assuming that we should be ashamed of sex itself. Wherever this idea came from, I can assure you it wasn't the Bible.

If you are tempted to think that God is horrified by sex or that he only allows it so that children can be born, let me take you back once more to the Garden of Eden. In Genesis 2:24, as God set down the pattern for marriage, we read that, 'a man leaves his father and mother and is united to his wife, and they become one flesh.'

According to the Bible, sex (becoming 'one flesh') was part of God's design even before Adam and Eve rebelled against him and brought sin into the world. If it existed in the perfection of the garden, where everything was completely untouched by the brokenness we see around us, then sex – as God created it – must be good.

If you are in still in doubt, have a look at the Song of Songs. One of my friends told me that the first time she read the intimate details of this sexual relationship between two lovers, she found herself wondering if someone had slipped it into the Bible without God noticing. I laughed but I knew what she meant. In a world where sex is often twisted into something it was never meant to be, it's easy to get the idea that God views it with disapproval or even disgust. Of course, God knows that this extraordinary love story is in the Bible. He put it there intentionally, in all its intimacy and sexual detail, so that we would understand that sex is part of his plan for marriage and that it is good.

If sex was simply designed to produce children, God could just as easily have made it a boring or even unpleasant duty. He didn't. He designed it to be enjoyable. When you are attracted to someone, it's not just in your mind. God created us with bodies that respond to each other in ways that bring us physical pleasure. When we enjoy each other as he intended, we honour the gift he has given us.

Myth 2: Sex is just something you do with your body

One of the reasons we talked about covenants before we came to this chapter is that, in the Bible, sex and the making of a covenant cannot be separated. When we try and split them apart, we lose something incredibly beautiful.

Do you remember how the different signs and images used during Old Testament covenant ceremonies helped people understand the importance of the promises they were making? In a similar way, the sexual relationship between a husband and wife doesn't just seal the marriage covenant; it also creates a vivid image. It reminds the couple, again and again, that their lives are joined in a bond deeper and more powerful than anything they can see with their eyes and feel in their bodies. What is happening physically is good but it's only part of the story.

In 1 Corinthians 6:16 Paul puts it like this: 'There's more to sex than mere skin on skin. Sex is as much spiritual mystery as physical fact. As written in Scripture, "The two become one."'[3] The fact that sex is so much more than just a physical experience gives it a richer beauty. It also means that if we choose to use it carelessly, the potential damage to ourselves and to others goes so much deeper.

I remember someone explaining this at our youth group using coloured paper. Two shapes were cut out and glued together, creating one new shape with two different coloured sides. When the glue had dried, we were told to try and separate the shapes. It took time but eventually we managed to rip them apart. The problem was that neither shape was the same as it had been when we started. Both pieces were curled up and torn in places, and each had patches of the other colour still attached.

The purpose of this illustration was to highlight that the bond created by sex is designed to be permanent – as part of a marriage covenant. When we join ourselves to someone in a sexual relationship, even temporarily, we share something that we can never fully take back.

Myth 3: If you really love someone, it's ok to have sex – you don't have to wait until you are actually married

One of my favourite things about winter is coming home on a cold day and lighting the little stove in our living room. There is something incredibly comforting about the dancing flames and the crackle of the logs as the heat from the fire starts to fill the room and thaw my frozen toes.

For a long time one of my daughters did not share my feelings. When she was very young, she had watched a movie in which a family lost their home in a fire. For years afterwards, every time we lit the stove or even burned a candle, we had to reassure her that our house was not going to burn down. Now that she's fifteen, she loves to light scented candles when she's studying and she's usually first to suggest we light the stove on a cold day (and the first to mention hot chocolate!). However, I have noticed that she is also the one who goes round the house at night, checking the candles have been blown out and the stove is properly closed. She may not be scared of fire anymore but she does have a healthy respect for it. As she knows how powerful it is and the damage it can do, she is careful to protect herself and the people she loves.

The powerful bond that sex creates is one of the reasons why God is so clear about the boundaries he places on it. The same God who loves us so much that he died to give us life designed our bodies to fully enjoy the gift of sex. He places it securely within a marriage relationship because he is loving, holy and knows what is good. When we find someone to share our lives with, he wants us to be able to enjoy that relationship fully and without regret. If this mysterious act of becoming 'one flesh' was designed to seal and deepen a marriage covenant, then sex between two people who are not married to each other can never be what it was intended to be. It does not matter how attractive the person is or how much you claim to love each other; if sex takes place before marriage or outside of a marriage relationship, the simple fact is that there is no covenant to seal. Not only that but the power that was intended for good becomes a force that can damage and cause pain.

Myth 4: If you only have a sexual relationship with one person for your whole life, you are missing out

For some reason our culture has bought into the lie that you can't be satisfied with spending your life in a sexual relationship with just one person. Please believe me when I tell you that is absolutely, completely, totally and utterly untrue.

Think for a moment about the ballet dancers we talked about back in chapter five. As they anticipate the movements of their partner and dance in perfect step, it's almost as though they can read each other's minds. That kind of understanding takes time to grow. The more they dance together, the better it becomes.

In most other areas of life we happily accept that a new skill takes time to learn. When it comes to love and sex, the media would have us believe it is possible to fall into bed with someone you barely know and immediately have an experience of sheer bliss. Don't fall for the digitally enhanced, edited and carefully choreographed sex scenes that will tempt you to settle for something empty and unsatisfying. When the director yells cut and the lights go out, all that's left are two actors awkwardly shuffling to get dressed as quickly as they can.

This image of sex is a cheap imitation of something that is designed to be so much more, and robs us of an experience that can only be found in the reality of a deep, covenant relationship. Somehow we have managed to turn the idea of freedom upside down. True freedom isn't moving from one relationship to the next without any permanent commitment; it's being free to love completely and without fear or regret.

Just as real love takes time to grow, it is only within a committed, lifelong relationship that sex can be enjoyed to the full. The experience of learning together becomes part of the adventure, like a secret between the two of you that makes your relationship completely unique. When sex is based on love and experienced within the protection and safety of a marriage commitment, there is room for laughter, trust and an enjoyment of each other that deepens with the passing of time.

Myth 5: God's plan for relationships is boring

We've caught glimpses already of love as God intended it. I hope these have begun to convince you that his plan for relationships is anything but boring. Rather than being dull, the security of marriage gives you the freedom to be completely comfortable with the other person in a way that means you can enjoy each other fully, without embarrassment or fear of rejection. When you commit to sharing your life with the person you love, following God together, you embark on an adventure that has purpose, direction and meaning – even when it's difficult. If that's considered boring, I'm ok with it. In fact, I'm all for it!

I believe without hesitation or doubt that deep, permanent covenant relationships are worth waiting for. Having said that, I need to warn you that pursuing love like this is not an easy choice. Following God wholeheartedly in any area of life means being intentional about the choices you make and the decision to walk closely with him. Relationships are no different. If you are serious about committing to trust God with any relationship you may have in the future, it will affect the decisions you make now.

In a world where all kinds of images are available at the click of a button, it means being careful even now about the things that you allow to shape your mind. If you make the decision to date, it's important to remember the powerful feelings that are part of being human do not magically switch on during a wedding ceremony. If you are going to be attracted to the person you marry, you'll be attracted to them long before you walk down the aisle.

Loving God and loving the other person will mean making decisions you stick to even when your body is telling you to go with your feelings. It may also mean being honest with yourself about the natural desires you feel and being careful not to put yourself in a position where resisting those feelings becomes almost impossible. This isn't easy and you will need to rely on God, but it's so worth it in the long run.

As we finish this chapter, we need to remember two important truths. The first is that God offers forgiveness when we fail. If you have already made mistakes in this area, it doesn't mean your life is ruined or that you can't have a good relationship in the future. God is good and compassionate, and he can bring healing and restoration to our lives in ways we can't imagine.

The second is less popular but equally true. Despite the wonderful truth of God's grace, the reality is that going against the commands of a God who is holy and loving will mean dealing with consequences that he never wanted for us. Obedience is *always* the best choice. It may be that as you discuss the contents of this chapter and explore the Bible further, you make some decisions about how you are going to approach dating. If this is the case, write them down in your journal as a commitment you can come back to in the future.

Finally, flip to the back of the book, where you will find a prayer for dating that was specially adapted from one of my favourite books, *Every Moment Holy* by Douglas Kaine McKelvey. It is a great reminder that the person you date is loved and valued by God, and that the decisions you make – individually and as a couple – are part of a bigger story.

Take a few moments to read through it now as you consider any decisions you may make about relationships. If you do date, now or in the future, you may find it helpful to come back to this prayer. It's a good way to remind yourself of the importance of honouring both God and the other person in every area of your relationship.

Questions

- If there was one thing about sex itself that you find confusing or would like to know more about, what would it be?
- According to the Bible, why can sex only be properly understood as part of a marriage covenant?
- In what ways can sex outside of or before marriage cause damage?
- How might the things you watch or think about impact the decisions you make about sex? What could you do to help protect your mind?

Think about

- Was there anything in this chapter that you found difficult to understand? If so, what was it?
- What did you learn from this chapter that you hadn't thought about before?
- Can you think of one question you have after reading this chapter?

Digging deeper

- Genesis 2:24–25 (Adam and Eve become 'one flesh').
- Song of Songs 7:6–12 (a groom and bride describe each other). Ephesians 5:1–3 (we are to live as children of God).
- Hebrews 13:4 (marriage should be honoured).
- 1 John 1:9 (God forgives us).

8

THE POWER OF HOME

BEFORE MY HUSBAND and I got married, we spent some time decorating the house we were going to share. It wasn't particularly fancy. Until we had curtains, there was a blanket taped in the window. The red living-room walls and blue kitchen worktop were pretty awful. Even so, it was ours and we loved it.

We talked a lot about paint colours, sofas and the carpet in the hallway but, looking back now, I realise we didn't spend much time planning the kind of home we were going to have. Let me explain what I mean by that.

When I was first married, I saw home as a place where Glenn and I could rest and be comfortable. It was somewhere we could retreat from everything that we did on the other side of our front door. I hoped that someday we would have children and I even wondered how we would decorate their bedrooms.

There was nothing wrong with those things; we did have children and in many ways our home is a place to rest and escape. However, I don't think I fully understood that the home we were building together was meant for more.

My favourite stories have always been C.S. Lewis' *The Chronicles of Narnia*. Thirty-five years after I first read them, they still capture my imagination in a way that feels both magical and deeply true. In *The Lion, the Witch and the Wardrobe*, there is a wonderful scene that takes place shortly after the children enter the magical world of Narnia. As they trudge through the snow, they come across Mr Beaver who takes them home to meet his wife. The Beaver's cottage is simple but they are welcomed as friends. The fire is warm and Mr and Mrs Beaver happily share what they have.

In the safety of the cottage, over a meal of potatoes, fish, tea and steaming marmalade roll, the children learn about Aslan for the first time. Even before they hear his story, just the mention of the name of the true King of Narnia changes the way they feel. Peter feels suddenly 'brave and adventurous' and Susan feels 'as if some delicious smell or music had just floated by her'. Lucy's response has always been my favourite. When Aslan's name is spoken, she gets 'the feeling you have when you wake up in the morning and realize that it is the beginning of the holidays or the beginning of summer.'[4]

Our world can be a difficult, confusing, heartbreaking place. There are times when people need a safe place to sit among friends and shelter from the storm. They need to hear the story of the true King whose name breathes hope into broken hearts, whispering the promise that winter is coming to an end and evil will be defeated.

A couple of summers ago our family was invited to stay with a friend whose gift for making her home welcoming and beautiful is legendary. I had shown my daughters pictures of the farmhouse in Georgia where she lives with her husband. I had told them the stories about the peacocks that roam in the grounds and the beautiful tea trays she is rumoured to set for her guests in the mornings. A couple of months before our visit I got a phone call to say that a devastating fire had almost destroyed their home and it was going to take at least a year to rebuild.

We did get to see them but our visit turned out very differently to the one we had planned. The evening was spent in a camper in the grounds of their burnt-out home. Most of what they had was borrowed and an injury to my friend's back meant she could barely move. Perhaps surprisingly that evening was one of the highlights of our trip. The meal was simple but it felt like a banquet as we talked and laughed (and cried a little), sharing the reality of a life that sometimes takes twists and turns you aren't expecting. When everything was stripped away, it turned out that the true beauty of her home wasn't in the elegant tea sets. It was in the reality of the love she shared with her husband, the warmth of the welcome they gave to others and, most importantly, their unshakeable hope in the God who was as present in the camper as he was in the beautiful farmhouse.

Over the years I have been welcomed into several homes that stand out in my memory. Whether the home of a single friend, or a family, or a couple with or without children, they are places where both laughter and tears are shared, forgiveness is offered, love is evident and God's presence is so real that it's impossible to miss. When I find myself in a place like that, it does two things. First, it helps me better understand who God is and the way he loves his people. Second, it makes me want to have that kind of home myself.

In the last chapter we thought about the way God designed our bodies to enjoy the sexual relationship that is part of marriage. You may have noticed that there was one important result of that relationship that we didn't really mention. In God's remarkable design sex does not only bring pleasure and form part of the bond between a couple. It can also lead to the birth of children and the beginning of a new family.

Deuteronomy 6 is one of my favourite chapters in the whole Bible. As the Israelites prepared to go into the land God had promised them, they were reminded that home and family would be right at the heart of teaching each new generation about God. If a couple were going to share this responsibility, then it was essential that both the husband and wife were committed to knowing God's word individually and living out the truth of it together. Deuteronomy 6:4–9 says:

Hear, O Israel: the LORD our God, the LORD is one. Love the LORD your God with all your heart and with all your soul and with all your strength. These commandments that I give you today are to be on your hearts. Impress them on your children. Talk about them when you sit at home and when you walk along the road, when you lie down and when you get up. Tie them as symbols on your hands and bind them on your foreheads. Write them on the door-frames of your houses and on your gates.

These verses paint a picture of something that feels a little like the conversations the children in Narnia had with Mr Beaver. For the Israelites, passing the beauty and truth of God's word on to the next generation meant his presence had to be a natural part of everyday family life, from the moment they woke up until the moment they went to sleep again. Parents were told to 'impress' the word of God on their children, not only teaching them what it meant but also demonstrating how to live it out. As they walked along the road, it wouldn't be unusual for his name to come up in the conversation. Perhaps as they travelled to celebrate Passover, they would tell the story of the rescue from Egypt. An argument between brothers might lead to a story about Joseph and his brothers. A beautiful sunset might spark a conversation about God as the Creator of the world. As they sat down to share a meal, the presence of God among them would be real, not because it was forced but because their story had been shaped by his.

God wanted his people to know him, understanding both his holiness and his love. Sometimes we make the mistake of assuming that the more difficult parts of the Bible, and maybe the Old Testament laws in particular, are irrelevant and dull. This couldn't be farther from the truth. The detailed interest God took in the everyday lives of his people was astonishing. Far from being boring, his laws helped them understand who he was and the kind of people he wanted them to be. Obedience to God's commands would mean living lives that were marked by holiness and love, radically different from the nations around them.

Keeping God's word at the heart of everyday life was so important that the Israelites were told to tie his commandments to their foreheads and arms, and write them on the doorposts and gates of their homes. That might seem a bit strange to us but these practical reminders were designed to help God's people keep his word at the centre of everything they thought, said or did. We may not physically tie God's word to our bodies (although some people do wear wristbands or other jewellery as a reminder of their commitment to follow God) but the principle is the same. As God's people, his word is never meant to be an add-on; it is the foundation on which we should build our lives.

Later in the same chapter Moses told the Israelites what would happen when they lived out these commands. Children, watching the hope and obedience of their parents, would ask why they lived the way they did. Parents would respond by telling their children the story of God's faithfulness to them and his love for his people. The key to understanding what it means to live like this is Deuteronomy 6:6: 'These commandments that I give you today are to be *on your hearts* (my italics).' If God's people were going to build homes where the character of God was evident and his word was taught and understood, they had to know him closely and personally. It's very hard to tell someone a story if you don't know it yourself.

I think one of the saddest verses in the Bible is Judges 2:10. God had done amazing things for his people, leading them into the Promised Land and defeating their enemies so they could live there in safety. Even so, we read these words: 'After that whole generation had been gathered to their fathers, another generation grew up who knew neither the LORD nor what he had done for Israel.' Despite God's faithfulness, it seems that this story was not passed on to the next generation. The consequences of that were disastrous then, and they are equally disastrous now.

It's easy to become so focused on what is happening in our lives, right here in this moment, that we lose sight of the fact that we are part of something bigger. 1 Peter 2:9 puts it like this: 'But you are a chosen people, a royal priesthood, a holy nation, God's special possession, that you may declare the praises of him who called you out of darkness into his wonderful light.'

Wonderful as they are, even romantic love, marriage and family were not created simply for our happiness and comfort. They were also designed to help us in the task of sharing the story of a God who is real with a world that is longing for hope. Whether we are passing that story on to the next generation or allowing the reality of his presence to shape homes that shine like beacons of light in a dark world, the character of the person we share the task with is important.

When we understand what is at stake and have a vision of the kind of home we want to build someday, it will make us think carefully about who we choose to share our lives with.

Questions

- In what ways might a Christian home be like the Beaver's cottage mentioned at the start of the chapter?
- When you think about the home you might have someday, what is important to you? Has that changed in any way after reading this chapter?
- Read 1 Peter 3:15. How might a home where God's presence is real and his love is evident cause people to ask questions?
- If a couple share the responsibility to live out God's love in their home and teach his word to their children, how would that affect your choice of the person you share your life with?

Think about

- Was there anything in this chapter that you found difficult to understand? If so, what was it?
- What did you learn from this chapter that you hadn't thought about before?
- Can you think of one question you have after reading this chapter?

Digging deeper

- Deuteronomy 6 (the need to teach the next generation God's word).
- Judges 2:10 (the consequences if God's word is not passed on).
- Luke 10:38, Acts 16:14–15 and 18:24–26 (examples of homes used for encouraging others and telling God's story).

9

A MAN AFTER GOD'S OWN HEART

A FEW MONTHS ago a visiting speaker told my church the story of his romance with the girl who eventually became his wife. When he first met her, they were both at college. He was immediately smitten. She felt the same way about him and it soon became obvious that a romance was beginning. That part of the story is not unusual. What I found interesting was the conversation they had before they began to date. The speaker explained that, even as a teenager, he had always believed God might call him to go overseas as a missionary. Knowing this, he sat down with the girl he had fallen for and explained that their relationship couldn't go any further unless she too was prepared to consider mission work as a possibility in the future.

Without meeting the man, it would be easy to read this story and imagine that he was demanding the girl he loved should become something she wasn't – just to please him or fit into his schedule. It wasn't like that at all. His respect and admiration for her was clear in the way he spoke about her. The love that was still so obvious decades later made that early conversation all the more remarkable. Despite his strong feelings, he considered obedience to God so important that he was not prepared to start dating someone who couldn't share the life he believed God was calling him to live. As important as his love for her was, his love for God mattered even more.

That's the kind of brave, daring commitment to God we are going to think about in this chapter. Maybe you are thinking, 'But I don't want to go overseas as a missionary! I don't even know what I want to do when I'm older.' While you may not know exactly what God is calling you to do with your life, that doesn't change the kind of person he wants you to be. Yes, it's exciting to discover the specific gifts you have been given and the role you might have in his story. In many ways, though, the details are less important than the desire to become more like Jesus and live a life that shows the world what he is like. If you are serious about following God, then that commitment will also mean thinking seriously about the kind of man you want to share your life with.

In the light of all we have talked about so far, the first and most obvious point is that it just doesn't make sense for someone who is committed to following God to choose to marry or even date someone who doesn't share their faith.

In 2 Corinthians 6:14 Paul writes to the church in Corinth, 'Do not be yoked together with unbelievers.' That may seem like a strange expression to us but the illustration is helpful. Let me explain.

When God was preparing the Israelites to go into the Promised Land, lots of the instructions he gave them were to do with practical, everyday life. One of the laws in Deuteronomy 22:10 concerned the way they farmed their fields. (Stick with me, there is a point to this!) To plough a field, two animals would be placed side by side and a long, curved piece of wood – called a yoke – would be placed on their shoulders. As they pulled the plough together, the weight would be shared between them and the ploughing would be easier and more effective. In order to work together properly, it was important that the animals were the same. If a donkey and an ox were 'yoked' together, the job became much harder than it needed to be and the lines they ploughed would be all over the place.

When the Christians in Corinth heard Paul's instruction, they understood the point he was making. The illustration can be applied in various areas of life but the most obvious one is relationships. It may not be romantic to compare marriage to two oxen pulling a plough. (I wouldn't recommend putting it on a Valentine's card.) However, it does help us understand why it is so important to choose to share your life with someone who can work side by side with you in the work to which you have been called.

Some things in the Bible are tricky to get your head

around but this isn't one of them. It amazes me how good we can be at convincing ourselves that the situation we are in is a special exception. We know what is true and yet we find ourselves adding a *but* …

Well, I know he's not actually following God but …
… he respects my faith and he supports my decision to follow God.
… I think he's really interested in God and he might become a Christian.
… there are so few committed Christian guys about.
… we love each other.

Convincing as these arguments might appear to be, they don't change the fact that choosing to start a romantic relationship with someone who doesn't share your faith in God is a really bad idea. What's more it is specifically going against God's instructions – no matter how good looking they are; no matter how much you like being around them; no matter how much they make you laugh.

It's so easy to get swept away by how good it is to be noticed and appreciated, and by the way someone makes you feel. But this area is too crucial to mess around with. That's why it's so important to think now about what matters most to you and to make wise decisions that you are more likely to stick to in the future.

There are two things I want you to understand before we go any further. First, please believe me when I tell you that this is not an attempt to put down people in your life who have not trusted God. Neither is it a suggestion that we should exclude those who are not Christians from our lives. That would be completely against God's command to love people as he loves them.

Second, I'm not suggesting that a marriage between two people who aren't Christians can't be a good marriage, or even that a marriage can't last when one person comes to faith and the other doesn't.

Instead, I'm talking about the situation where a person is committed to following God and is not yet married. They have the opportunity to choose to spend their life with someone who can share fully in God's plans for them; someone who enjoys the unique intimacy of a shared relationship with God.

To help you understand why that is worth holding out for, here's a recap of some key points we have discovered so far about love and marriage. As you read them, take a moment to think about what would happen in each case if the person you share your life with doesn't know God. What would the problems be?

- Part of the adventure of marriage is combining your strengths and working to serve God together. Love means committing to put the other person first and think about their needs before your own.
- Romantic love, as God intended it, includes the responsibility to help your husband or wife get to know God better and become more like Jesus.

- When you have a sexual relationship with someone, that joining together is a sign that you have become part of each other in a way that is much deeper than just a physical bond. When you build a home together, you share the responsibility to create a place where God's kingdom is lived out. This is where children (if you have them) are to grow up hearing God's story and watching how it shapes everyday life.

When you consider how seriously God takes the responsibility of husbands and wives to love each other, even when it's difficult, the importance of sharing your life with someone who knows God personally becomes even clearer.

In Ephesians 5 wives are told to support and respect their husbands. For a long time I only thought about what that verse meant for me. It wasn't until I looked closely at the responsibility of husbands that I saw it in a different light. According to Paul, husbands are told to show their wives the same love that Jesus showed the church, stopping at nothing to love her fully and completely, even if that means sacrificing himself. *That's a big ask for husbands!* But how much easier it is for a wife to respect and support someone who loves her like that! It's not so difficult to love someone who wants you to become the very best version of yourself, follows God with passion, and uses all their skills to help both of you know God better and serve him together.

For a husband to love like that will require a real relationship with God. This goes way beyond raising your hand in church when you are seven to say you have accepted Jesus and then carrying on for the rest of your life as though nothing has changed. It is only made possible by walking closely with God and loving in response to the incredible, selfless love that God has shown to us.

2 Corinthians 3:18 tells us that when we enter into a covenant relationship with God, his desire is that we are changed to become more and more like him. That is the case whoever we are and whatever position we find ourselves in. It's God's desire both for you and for the person you may eventually marry.

It's not enough to be able to say the right things. Loving God means living a life that begins to show the change that is taking place within us.

In John 13–15 Jesus mentions three things that will act as proof that someone is genuinely his disciple. They are a good way of looking at our own lives and testing our relationship with God. If you are considering dating someone, they might also help you look beyond your feelings for a moment and think seriously about whether that person is walking with God.

Proof 1: 'By this everyone will know that you are my disciples, if you love one another' (John 13:35)

If we truly love God, then that love will affect how we treat other people. Whether they are parents or siblings, friends, or even strangers we meet on the bus, becoming like Jesus means treating others like he does.

Proof 2: 'Whoever has my commands and keeps them is the one who loves me' (John 14:21)
If we love God, we will be committed to getting to know the Bible and living lives that are shaped by obedience to God's word. This commitment to obedience doesn't mean we will get it right all the time but it does mean we will care when we realise we have done things that go against God's word. Holiness matters to God and it should matter to us.

Proof 3: 'This is to my father's glory, that you bear much fruit, showing yourselves to be my disciples' (John 15:8)
If we are walking with God, our lives will show evidence of his presence within us. Galatians 5:22 tells us that the fruit the Holy Spirit produces in our lives is 'love, joy, peace, forbearance [patience], kindness, goodness, faithfulness, gentleness and self-control.'

I think it's worth adding that although these proofs can be a really helpful guide, there is a danger here. We could use them to create a checklist for finding the perfect guy and forget something really important along the way: *becoming like Jesus is a work in progress*. Abraham and David were known for their close relationships with God. Abraham was called 'God's friend' (James 2:23) and God called David 'a man after my own heart' (Acts 13:22). This is all the more amazing (and extremely encouraging) because in reality even Abraham and David messed up in some pretty spectacular ways.

Finding a guy who loves God does not mean he won't make mistakes. Just as there is no such thing as the perfect girl, there is no such thing as the perfect guy. We are still part of a broken world. While the brokenness remains, none of us will be able to perfectly reflect the heart of God.

However, *and this is vitally important*, there is a difference between a guy who messes up sometimes but loves and genuinely wants to obey God, and a guy who shows no desire to know God or obey his word. Sharing your life with someone who loves God but makes mistakes will require the same forgiveness, encouragement and grace that God shows you. Wonderfully, as the person you love offers the same forgiveness and grace to you, you will find that you are actually teaching each other to be more like Jesus. On the other hand, if *none* of these proofs are evident, that might be a pretty good indication that this is a relationship you do not want to get involved in.

There is one last thing that I want to mention. If people in your life who care about you are worried about a relationship you are in, listen to what they have to say. I'm not suggesting that your parents, siblings, youth workers or even good friends will always be right about who you should date or marry. But if they know and love you, and are brave enough to share their genuine concerns, do yourself a favour and listen. Strong feelings have a way of making us blind to truth we don't want to see. Sometimes the people who love us can see things more clearly than we can. It may be that you don't agree with them in the end, but have the courage to think seriously and pray about what they are saying. You may well end up saving yourself a lot of heartache.

Questions

- How important do you think it is to marry someone who shares your faith? Why? What difference does it make?
- Do you think the same standards apply to dating? Why or why not?
- If you are in a relationship with someone who is a Christian, how important do you think it is that they are living a life that demonstrates their commitment to God? Why?
- How might you tell the difference between someone who knows the right things to say and someone who is genuinely committed to following God?
- Read Micah 6:8 and Titus 2:6–8. What characteristics does God value in these verses? What do they look like in everyday life?

Think about

- Was there anything in this chapter that you found difficult to understand? If so, what was it?
- What did you learn from this chapter that you hadn't thought about before?

- Can you think of one question you have after reading this chapter?

Digging deeper

- Deuteronomy 10:12–13 (what God wants his people to be like).
- Ephesians 5:22–33 (instructions on the relationship between husbands and wives).
- Psalm 51 (David's response to his own sin).

10

FORGIVENESS

A COUPLE OF years ago, while I was ironing some clothes and not paying too much attention to what was going on around me, my daughter asked a question that caught me by surprise: 'Mum, do you ever get fed up with Dad?'

My immediate response was to smile, give her a quick hug and reassure her that I never got tired of her father. The problem was that I was lying, and the look on her face as she turned to leave the room told me she knew that. Swallowing hard, I called her back, apologised and began to tell her the truth.

I love my husband. I really do. He's a great husband and a great dad. He encourages me to be myself, he makes me laugh, he's always quick to say he's sorry and most importantly he loves God deeply. He's also different from me in a lot of ways:

- He's an extrovert; I'm an introvert.
- He likes noise; I like silence.
- He loves football; I prefer books.
- He makes decisions before he speaks; I tend to think out loud.

These are just a few examples. Most of the time our differences are a good thing, but some days they make it hard to be in the same room without having an argument.

Not long after we got married, I discovered something that no one had told me before: no matter how much you love someone, there will be times when the person who once made your heart race will drive you crazy. It doesn't mean you married the wrong person or that you have 'fallen out of love'; it just means you are human.

In the interest of honesty, I should tell you that I have found it difficult to write some parts of this book. I believe that the Bible is true. In fact, the better I get to know God – and the older I become – the more convinced I am that his way is always the best way. He knows us better than anyone, his heart is kinder than we could ever dare to imagine and he always wants the best for us. If he asks us to do hard things, it is because he sees the bigger picture and he knows the end result will be worth it.

Sadly, knowing this doesn't mean I always get it right. Sometimes I judge and speak harshly when love would have been better shown through kindness. I put myself first and hurt the people I wanted to love. Too often I get mad when God is asking me to forgive.

You may have heard this expression: 'Love means never having to say you are sorry.' That might sound appealing but it couldn't be further from the truth. Pride might mean never saying you are sorry but love means saying it over and over again, as often as you fail.

The reality of being broken people in a broken world means that part of love is learning to forgive and be forgiven. The people we love are flawed and human just like us. Sooner or later they will do things that irritate us, disappoint us or cause us pain. Sometimes they will be small things but other times the hurt is deeper and more difficult to deal with. The question is how should we respond as followers of Jesus? The answer is much easier to write than it is to live.

In Ephesians 4:32 Paul says, 'Be kind and compassionate to one another, forgiving each other, just as in Christ God forgave you.' In the same way, our love for others should be a response to the love of God. Understanding the forgiveness God has shown to us – and allowing his grace to change our hearts – will make it possible to forgive others.

If we want to understand forgiveness, we have to start with Jesus.

The religious leaders of Jesus' time were not happy with the way he taught God's law. They couldn't argue with his knowledge – he knew it inside out – but he taught it with kindness and authority, explaining the heart behind it in a way that people had never heard before. It drove the religious leaders crazy and they were desperate to find a way to catch him out.

In John 8:1–11 we read the story of a woman who had broken the law by having a sexual relationship with a man who was not her husband. Back then this was punishable by death. The religious leaders saw a perfect opportunity to trap Jesus. If he agreed with the law, the woman would be stoned to death but the compassion that drew people to him would be thrown into doubt. On the other hand, if he let her go, he would be saying that God's holy standards weren't really important. Dragging the woman into the temple courts, the religious leaders stood her in front of Jesus, demanding that he decide what should be done with her.

Can you imagine how the woman must have felt?

The temple courts are packed and she lowers her gaze to avoid the judgment in the eyes of the crowd. Their looks of disgust are like arrows that pierce her already broken heart. The man she had the relationship with is nowhere to be seen. Her legs are trembling so violently that she has to fight to stay on her feet. She waits, terrified, for the death sentence she knows is coming.

While she tries desperately to shut out the angry taunts of her accusers, Jesus bends down and begins to write on the ground with his finger. *What is he doing?*

As the crowd turn their attention to Jesus, she dares to glance up. No one is looking at her anymore. The shouts have changed. 'What's he writing?' 'Can you see what he is doing?'

A hush falls over the crowd as Jesus slowly stands up and looks her accusers in the eye. 'Let any one of you who is without sin be the first to throw a stone at her.'

Silence.

He bends down again and she braces herself against the pain. *Let it be over quickly.*

But the stones don't come. Instead, she hears footsteps. There are more and more of them until eventually her accusers are gone and she is left alone with Jesus.

This time when he straightens up, he looks right at her. His eyes are warm and deep, and they seem to see straight into her soul. His voice is strong and firm and yet soft with kindness.

> *'Woman, where are they? Has no one condemned you?'*
>
> *'No one, sir,' she said.*
>
> *'Then neither do I condemn you,' Jesus declared. 'Go now and leave your life of sin' (John 8:10–11).*

That's the heart of the God who calls you his beloved daughter.

When Jesus offered forgiveness, it wasn't because the woman's sin didn't matter. He understood the full cost of her sin (and the sins of those who stood there accusing her), but he was able to forgive her because he knew the penalty for it was going to be paid. Holiness meant the death sentence would still be handed down. Love meant Jesus would stand in her place, giving his life in exchange for hers.

It wouldn't be long before the people who had pointed their fingers and shouted for this woman's blood would turn their attention to Jesus. This time no one would write in the dust. The eyes of all heaven and earth would stay fixed on him as he hung there, naked and vulnerable, carrying the weight of her sin.

And my sin.

And your sin.

That's the forgiveness our God offers. He does not turn a blind eye to our mistakes but, looking at the cross, declares we are free to go because the penalty has already been paid.

Our God is holy and awesome, and he calls us to live lives that are worthy of his kingdom. But he doesn't hand down rules and then sit back and judge us on how well we keep them. He doesn't turn his back on us when the circumstances we find ourselves in, or the choices we make in our brokenness, leave us in a pain he never wanted us to feel. Our sin and rebellion against God are serious and they have to be dealt with, but he loves us so deeply and so completely that he died to make sure they never have to separate us from him again.

How does it make you feel to know you've been forgiven like that? Does it have any effect on the way you treat other people?

Peter had spent time with Jesus and so he knew that love goes hand in hand with extravagant forgiveness. One day he came to Jesus with a question: 'Lord, how many times shall I forgive my brother or sister who sins against me? Up to seven times?' (Matthew 18:21).

That seems pretty generous, doesn't it? Forgiving someone once is hard. Forgiving the same person twice is harder. Peter was not only prepared to forgive but was willing to do it seven times. Maybe he thought Jesus would be impressed with his generosity. He wasn't.

Jesus answered, 'I tell you, not seven times, but seventy-seven times' (Matthew 18:22). By this he wasn't saying Peter should keep a tally until he got to seventy-six and then give the person their final warning. He was telling Peter to stop counting and forgive without limits. To help Peter understand why he was asked to be so generous with his forgiveness, Jesus told this story:

> *The kingdom of God is like a king who decided to square accounts with his servants. As he got under way, one servant was brought before him who had run up a debt of a hundred thousand dollars. He couldn't pay up, so the king ordered the man, along with his wife, children, and goods, to be auctioned off at the slave market.The poor wretch threw himself at the king's feet and begged, 'Give me a chance and I'll pay it all back.' Touched by his plea, the king let him off, erasing the debt.The servant was no sooner out of the room when he came upon one of his fellow servants who owed him ten dollars. He seized him by the throat and demanded, 'Pay up. Now!' The poor wretch threw himself down and begged, 'Give me a chance and I'll pay it all back.' But he wouldn't do it. He had him arrested and put in jail until the debt was paid. When the other servants saw this going on, they were outraged and brought a detailed report to the*

> *king. The king summoned the man and said, 'You evil servant! I forgave your entire debt when you begged me for mercy. Shouldn't you be compelled to be merciful to your fellow servant who asked for mercy?' The king was furious and put the screws to the man until he paid back his entire debt. And that's exactly what my Father in heaven is going to do to each one of you who doesn't forgive unconditionally anyone who asks for mercy.*[5]

When you read this, it's hard to believe that someone could be so unfair. Imagine being let off with a debt of $100,000 and then having your friend thrown into prison because they couldn't pay you back the $10 they owed! *Who would do that?*

It turns out I would.

When we accept the forgiveness God offers us and yet refuse to forgive others, we behave in exactly the same way as the servant who had been forgiven the enormous debt. If we really understand what God has done for us, letting it sink in and change our hearts, it affects the way we treat others. Like love, forgiveness is not optional for those who want to walk closely with God.

If you find it difficult to forgive, the good news is that forgiveness, like love, is a choice that goes beyond feelings. Forgiving as God forgives is not about pretending that nothing happened or that the hurt is not real. It's not even about ignoring the practical consequences of sin. Psalm 103:12 tells us: 'as far as the east is from the west, so far has he removed our transgressions from us.' If God has chosen to remove our sin completely, then forgiveness means choosing not to keep dragging up the past and punishing the other person ourselves. The fact that forgiveness is a choice makes it possible even when we are still feeling hurt or disappointed. We might not be able to stop the memories popping up but we can choose not to act on them, and not to keep reliving them in our minds, until eventually our feelings catch up. The surprising thing is that sometimes when we deal with hard things, and are able to forgive and move on, the relationship gets stronger as a result.

That's true in marriage just as it is true in any other relationship. When we learn to forgive our friends and family now, we are obeying God and showing others his heart, as well as training ourselves to love well later.

According to Micah 7:18, God not only forgives us but delights to do so. When he asks us to forgive as he forgives, he is also asking us to do it willingly. Can you imagine what would happen if we lived with this attitude, not just forgiving each other grudgingly but being ready, willing and even glad to let go of one another's mistakes?

When we choose to love others by forgiving them and letting go of their failures, we show that we have understood the incredible, undeserved, complete and unlimited forgiveness that God has shown to us.

Questions

- What does it mean to forgive someone?
- How might it affect your relationships with your family or friends if you hold on to things that have happened in

the past or continually focus on the faults of the other person? How would it affect a romantic relationship?

- How does forgiving your family and friends now prepare you to love better later?
- Why does God forgive us?
- Read Matthew 6:14–15. How does it affect your relationship with God when you refuse to forgive the people in your life?

Think about

- Was there anything in this chapter that you found difficult to understand? If so, what was it?
- What did you learn from this chapter that you hadn't thought about before?
- Can you think of one question you have after reading this chapter?

Digging deeper

- Psalm 103:1–13 and Micah 7:18–19 (God's forgiveness to us).
- Luke 23:34 (Jesus asks his Father to forgive those who were crucifying him).
- John 8:1–11 (Jesus forgives the woman caught in adultery).
- Colossians 3:13 (we are to forgive each other).

11

SATISFIED IN GOD

ACCORDING TO ECCLESIASTES 3:11, God has placed within each one of us an awareness that we are made for more than just this life. Deep inside, whether we realise it or not, there is an ache for his presence that won't go away, no matter what we try to fill it with.

I used to think that being satisfied meant making do with what you had. If I wanted dessert but there wasn't any, my parents would say, 'Be satisfied with what you've got!' Being satisfied by God is not like that at all. He doesn't ask us to make do with him. When he comes into our lives, he wants to light us up inside. He fills us until we overflow with things that are true and good and completely unchanged by any circumstance we find ourselves in. If my daughters were to say they only had time to read one chapter in this book, that's why I would tell them to read this one. If we were created for God and can be satisfied only by him, that means nothing else can completely satisfy us, no matter how important it seems. Not career. Not achievement. Not popularity. Not wealth. Not even a relationship.

Sometimes we fool ourselves into believing that if we can just find the right person to love, we will be perfectly happy, fulfilled and complete. That is a dangerous idea for many reasons but let me point out three.

First, it may be that marriage is not part of God's plan for your life. If true satisfaction is found in romantic relationships, then singleness would be a disaster. *But* if God himself can satisfy you in a way that no one else ever could, and his plans for you are always good, then you can look to the future with confidence, wherever God leads you.

Second, if we spend our lives watching the horizon, desperately searching for our dream guy, the tragedy is that we miss the God who is right beside us, ready to give us the very satisfaction we are longing for.

Third, even if you do end up getting married, it's just as important to know that only God can fully answer the deep longing he has placed within you. Don't expect the person you marry to do that. While someone you love can bring you comfort and joy, sharing the experiences that life brings (both good and bad) – and encouraging you to know God better – the truth is that no human relationship can ever satisfy you completely. When you ask that of another person, you place a burden on them that they were never meant to carry.

In Psalm 63:3 David makes a radical claim. Despite the difficulty and struggle he was facing at that time, he says that the faithful, deep, love of God 'is better than life' itself. According to Jesus, knowing God is not just part of life; it *is* life (John 17:3). If we want to live the life we were created for, it can only be found in the presence of God. Not only will this last forever but it is infinitely richer and deeper now than anything we could create or experience without him.

If I had to pick a favourite psalm, I would choose Psalm 73, mostly because the writer's experience feels so familiar. At the beginning he looks around at the world he lives in and sees people who seem to be doing well, despite making decisions that go against God's word. In fact, they often seem to be doing better than those who are trying to do what God has asked of them. They mock God and make fun of his people, and no one steps in to make them stop. The psalmist wants to keep walking with God but his feet are slipping. His grip on all that God has called him to is getting loose. *Why bother struggling to live for God if it doesn't make a difference anyway?*

In the middle of the psalm is a moment when everything changes. As he comes into God's presence, the psalmist gets to see life from God's viewpoint. When he stops focusing on what is right in front of him and looks up, seeing instead the great and wonderful story that God is telling, he realises that there is more to life than what his eyes can see. He may have started by admitting that he was struggling to keep living for God but he finishes with these beautiful words:

Whom have I in heaven but you?
And earth has nothing I desire besides you.
My flesh and my heart may fail,
but God is the strength of my heart
and my portion for ever.

(Psalm 73:25–26)

For the psalmist, life only starts to make sense when it is seen through God's eyes. It's almost as if God has pulled back the curtain and let him catch a glimpse of all that is real and true. The truth that he finds in God's presence helps him put the struggles of everyday life into perspective. It doesn't stop the hard things being hard or the painful things being painful, but it reminds him that he is part of a story that will outlast anything he faces in this life.

I have a friend who (like me) grew up loving the *Anne of Green Gables* books. As a young adult, her dad took her to visit Prince Edward Island, where the stories took place. When my friend, a great storyteller herself, describes the experience of arriving on the island, it's easy to imagine yourself leaning over the railings of the ferry with the salty sea breeze blowing through your hair. I love listening to her talk about the moment she saw the beach for the first time. Looking down at the sand dunes she had walked through so often in her mind, heart thundering and eyes filling with tears, she shouted to her Dad, 'It's all here! It's exactly the way I imagined it!'

I wonder if that is a very small picture of how we will feel when we discover that the things God taught us here in our broken world have only been glimpses of something more wonderful and beautiful than anything we could dare to dream. If we can find our voices at all, maybe we'll shout, 'It's all true! Everything he promised us is true!'

There are things that God will only show you if you come to him and ask. In Jeremiah 33:3 he says, 'Call to me and I will answer you and tell you great and unsearchable things you do not know.' In his beautiful prayer in Ephesians, Paul prays that his friends will know God's love in a way that goes beyond what they can understand with just their minds (Ephesians 3:19).

There is a difference between knowing *about* God and knowing God. The first is information. The second (the kind of knowing Paul wants for his friends) is an intimate, life-changing relationship that grows in God's presence as we talk to him and get to know him through his word.

Within the pages of his word, God has shown me glimpses of his heart that have astonished me. When I first began to see how the Bible fits together, each book telling a different part of the same story of God's unstoppable love for his people, I encountered God in a whole new way. If you struggle to see the Bible as a story, you might find it helpful to read Sally Lloyd-Jones' wonderful book *The Story of God's Love for You.*[6] It is easy to read and it shows beautifully how the whole Bible is telling the story of who God is and how he has relentlessly pursued the people he loves.

One of the most important things I discovered in my late teens was that, like love and forgiveness, talking to God and studying the Bible is a choice that sometimes has to overrule your feelings. There have been many times in my life when I have regretted choosing, through my actions, not to put God first. I have given in to the strong pull of endless Netflix, constant social media and countless other distractions, and I have come away empty. In all the years I have been a Christian, I have never once regretted time spent alone with God. Gradually, despite my stumbling and failing, God has taught me to love his word.

Don't misunderstand me – I don't always wake up with a burning desire to read the Bible. Some days more than others it has to be an intentional choice. There are still many times when I struggle to understand difficult passages. Even if I live until I am an old woman, I will have barely begun to uncover the full wonder of God's love and holiness and grace. But there have been moments when I have sat with tears pouring down my face, completely overwhelmed by the beauty of who he is and what he has done for us. Moments like that change everything.

We live in a world where people are constantly told to look inside themselves to find out who they really are. According to Psalm 139:13, it was God who knit us together inside our mother's womb. He knows our thoughts and he knows what we will say before we even speak. He created us carefully and with a purpose, and he knows every detail of the life we haven't lived yet. The only way to find out who you truly are is by first getting to know the God who created you. That is important in life generally, and it's also important when it comes to relationships.

I have already said that part of marriage is combining your strengths and the gifts God has given you with those of your husband, then working together to play your part in God's story. The way to bring the best of ourselves to a marriage is by first discovering who we are in God.

That leaves us with a challenge. If we want to be satisfied in God, we have to be wise about what we choose to believe. If you spend all your time absorbing the messages that you will find on social media and on TV and movie screens, it is bound to affect the way you see yourself. In the last few years I have come across so many young girls who are crippled by the pressure that advertising and social media put on them. Constant images of girls with apparently perfect lives, boyfriends, faces and bodies chip away at their self-worth until they become a shadow of what God intended them to be.

Please, *please* don't allow yourself to be shaped by lies.

The truth is that, if you have trusted Jesus, you are a daughter of the Most High God, loved and cherished by him and perfectly equipped to play your part in his story. His love for you is not based on your skin or your dress size or your grades or your popularity, but on the fact that you are now – and forever will be – *his*. Open the Bible and let him show you the truth of who he is and who you really are. Find your worth in him. You won't regret it.

As you get to know God, let the truth of who he is and who you are in him influence everything, including your relationships. Let your love for him shape both *how* you choose to love and *who* you choose to love. If the time comes, let obedience to God lead you into a love that helps you become the very best version of yourself, sharing a lifetime of serving God with someone who loves you deeply but loves God even more.

- Someone who supports and understands the passions God has put on your heart.
- Someone who is committed to God's word and will encourage you to know God better.
- Someone you can make a deep, binding covenant with, enjoying every part of the love you share and being faithful to him for the rest of your life.
- Someone you can willingly support and encourage as you work side by side in the adventure God has called you to live.

There may be adventures in your future that are wonderful and exciting, just as there may be difficulty and heartache. Whatever life has in store, my prayer for you and for my own daughters is that God himself will always be your greatest love. You will stumble and fall, and you won't always get it right. But if you choose to follow him, he will hold you every step of the way. Only God knows what lies ahead. If you let him, he will use the journey to teach you to trust him and listen to his voice, getting you ready for anything or anyone that is waiting further down the road.

Questions

- Read Ephesians 1:17–20. What does Paul pray that God will do for the Ephesians? What three things does he want them to know?
- What does it mean to be satisfied in God?
- What's the difference between knowing about God and knowing God?
- What happens if you try to find all your happiness and satisfaction in another person?
- What could you do to help yourself spend time with God and get to know him better?

Think about

- Was there anything in this chapter that you found difficult to understand? If so, what was it?
- What did you learn from this chapter that you hadn't thought about before?
- Can you think of one question you have after reading this chapter?

Digging deeper

- Psalm 73 (come to God to make sense of life).

- Psalm 139 (we are created and known by God).
- Ephesians 3:16–21 (Paul prays that the Ephesians would know God).

A LITURGY FOR DATING OR COURTSHIP

By Douglas Kaine McKelvey

Here is where I am, O Lord –

I find myself drawn to one in whom I see
a lasting beauty,
a depth of soul,
a steady wisdom,
and a sensitivity to goodness and truth.

I praise you, God, for creating such a person
and displaying in them unique expression
of your glory.

I thank you that my path has crossed theirs
in this time and place in history.
I am increasingly drawn to this one you have
created, and I desire to know them more.

But I cannot see the path that lies ahead
on this journey toward eternity.
So give me wisdom, Lord.
Do not let my emotions get ahead of me.

In the time that I spend with this your beloved
child, let me not act selfishly. Let me not take
lightly my constant responsibility for the heart
and well-being of another, regardless of
my own momentary feelings and desires.

Let me remember that this relationship
does not affect only the two of us.
It exists inside a web of other
relationships with family and friends
who had already invested years
of nurture and care and love and prayer
and tears and delight in this person,
long before I ever met them.

So let me act now
and always in this relationship
in ways that would honor all
who love this person. Let me build
on that good foundation,
that whatever the two of us now create together
would be a blessing to all who know us.

Indeed O Lord, give us in these hours we share
the wisdom to build well,
that even if all we cultivate is a friendship,
it will still in its own humble way
be a source of encouragement and beauty
to those around us.

Or if we awaken one day to the understanding
that what we were creating all along
was not just a friendship,
but an enduring love – in which
the remainder of our lives
and the lives of our children and grandchildren
and all of our friendships and all
of our service to you, O God,
would be lived out together
in the bond of marriage – then all
the more reason we should build well
and with intentionality and unselfish love
here at the beginning.

Give me this wisdom, therefore.
Give me this grace.
Give me patience and an eternal perspective
that would govern well my choices today,
and in all the days to follow.

Do not let my emotions
get ahead of me, O Lord.
Let me love you by loving this person well,
and in kindness and self-restraint
let me always choose their greatest good
as if it were my own.

Amen.[7]

A LETTER TO PARENTS

DEAR PARENT,

If you are looking at the teenager in front of you and wondering how you got here so quickly or how you are meant to prepare her for all that lies ahead, then you and I are in the same boat. At the time of writing my daughters are thirteen and fifteen. I wrote this book because there are some things that I really want my girls to know. First, above anything else, I want them to know that they are already loved. The same God who created the heavens and the earth knows them intimately and loves them so completely that he was prepared to die in their place. They can't earn his love and they can't lose it. Their successes won't make him love them more and their failures won't make him love them less. They don't have to prove themselves or hide the truth of who they are. The love that he has for them is deeper and richer and more satisfying than any love they will find in their lifetime, no matter how wonderful that love might be.

Second, I want them to know that the choices they make are important. As they navigate life in a world that is becoming more and more confused about sex, sexuality and relationships in general, I desperately want my girls to catch a glimpse of something that is good, beautiful and true. This love is not only worth pursuing and working hard for but shapes the decisions they make when it comes to relationships, whatever age they are. If they do eventually marry, God's plan is a relationship that will bring out the best in them and draw them closer to him. I want them to choose the kind of love that helps them play their part in the greater story of God's redemption of our broken world.

I believe it's good to want these things because, according to the Bible, God wants them too.

It's important to point out that this book is primarily written for girls who have already chosen to follow God. We live in a world that is becoming increasingly hostile to the design for relationships found in the Bible. This is not an attempt to force biblical standards on people who do not believe in or follow God. Rather, it is designed as a resource to help girls who are trying to understand love as God designed it, and to figure out what it means to live as God has called them to do.

It has never been my plan that this book would answer every question your teen has about relationships. Instead, my goal is to help you start a conversation that will hopefully continue for years to come. I realise that some of the issues my daughters will face at eighteen and twenty will not be the same ones they are dealing with at thirteen and fifteen. Knowing that, I want it to be normal for us to have natural, honest conversations about issues as they arise, cultivating the habit of turning to God and his word as the guide in any decisions that are being made. My prayer is that this book will be part of that process, for us and for you.

When I first began to have conversations about relationships with my daughters, one of the biggest difficulties was figuring out where to start. I didn't want to just give them a book and leave them to read it alone. On the other hand, it felt like trying to cover everything in conversation could easily turn into a lecture. This book aims to find the middle ground between these approaches.

Each chapter can be read individually, giving both of you an opportunity to go through it at your own pace and think about the topics that are raised. At the end of the chapter there are some questions to discuss. The questions are just a guide and may not cover a particular issue the chapter has raised for your teen. That's ok. For that reason, each chapter also finishes with the same three *Think about* questions, intended to help raise any additional concerns, questions or thoughts which have come up after thinking through the chapter. I have encouraged readers to keep a journal handy so that they can privately jot down any questions they have, things they have learned or even decisions they have made around their own approach to relationships. Finally, there is an optional *Digging deeper* section at the end of each chapter with a couple of suggested Bible passages to help you get started if you want to explore the subject further.

Before you begin, I thought it might be helpful to share some of the struggles I have had while talking through the various chapters with my daughters. Should the same issues arise for you, it might be useful to have considered them in advance.

If I'm being honest, I don't find these conversations particularly easy. Writing about subjects like love, relationships and sex is one thing but looking into the face of my teen and answering hard questions is another thing entirely. Having said that, I have found that the more we talk, the easier it gets. As they share their struggles and ask questions, their bravery increases. As I answer honestly, mine does too. We have the occasional awkward moment, but as we persevere we're even learning to laugh at our discomfort.

For me the hardest times have been when what we are reading together doesn't match up to what my daughters see in my life. Marriage can be a wonderful adventure but some days it's also really, *really* hard. I believe that loving someone in the way God intends means putting them first, even when you don't feel like it. Sadly, in my own selfishness, I often do the opposite. My daughters know this. They know that I am not always gentle and kind when I speak, and they know that I don't always show the grace that God has shown to me.

Sometimes, in the course of writing this, I've had to be honest about that and apologise to them and to my husband. Admitting my own failure to always live out what I know to be true, while difficult, has turned into something positive. Not only has it challenged me but it has reminded my daughters that God uses broken people.

My prayer for my daughters, and for yours, is that they will choose to follow God and pursue real love – not because we have told them to, but because they have become so captivated by God and satisfied in him that they are prepared to trust him wholeheartedly with every area of their lives. I may not know you personally but I am praying that God will help you approach this important subject with wisdom, sensitivity, a little humour and a hunger for him that is infectious.

In him,
Heidi

NOTES

[1] S.D. Smith, *The Green Ember* (Story Warren Books, 2015).

[2] Sally Lloyd-Jones, *The Story of God's Love for You* (Zondervan, 2015).

[3] Eugene H. Peterson, *The Message Remix* (NavPress, 2003).

[4] C.S. Lewis, *The Lion, the Witch and the Wardrobe* (Collins, 1980).

[5] Matthew 18:21–35, from Eugene H. Peterson, *The Message Remix*.

[6] Sally Lloyd-Jones, *The Story of God's Love for You*.

[7] Douglas Kaine McKelvey, *Every Moment Holy* (Rabbit Room Press, 2017). Specially adapted from 'A Liturgy for Dating and Courtship', www.everymomentholy.com.

CHOOSING LOVE
IN A BROKEN WORLD
HEIDI JOHNSTON